C000150164

Clear and concise. This book will be
not quite sure where they stand wit
Mike Cain, Emmanuel, Bristol

I'm a Christian, Aren't I? is a book every young believer should read.
Dan Clark shows us very clearly the key components that make up
the jigsaw of the Christian life and roots it in real-life stories. After
reading this book you are left with no doubt that unless you have
all the jigsaw pieces in place you are selling yourself short on a full
authentic life in Jesus.
Charmaine Muir, All Souls, Langham Place

Dan Clark asks a simple and vital question, and in a straightforward
and accessible way he pieces together the Bible's answer. The last
chapter on the effects of missing some of these pieces is immensely
helpful. For anyone who needs confidence about their relationship
with God, the book is ideal. So that's pretty much all of us then!
Dominic Smart, Gilcomston South Church, Aberdeen

Dan Clark has written a very helpful book, which targets the
misconceptions that so often hinder people from finding a real faith
in Jesus Christ. Warm, easy to understand and accompanied by
personal testimonies which wonderfully illuminate what it really
means to grasp the gospel.
Rico Tice, All Souls, Langham Place

Dan Clark

I'm a Christian, aren't I?

Grasping the full picture

ivp

INTER-VARSITY PRESS
Norton Street, Nottingham NG7 3HR, England
Email: ivp@ivpbooks.com
Website: www.ivpbooks.com

The pen portraits that start each chapter and those included part way through the
introduction and conclusion are fictional, although many of them are based on a
mixture of what real people have said to me or others. All the other stories quoted
or put in boxes are definitely real!

First published 2010

British Library Cataloguing in Publication Data
A catalogue record for this book is available from the British Library.

ISBN: 978–1–84474–419–0

Typeset by CRB Associates, Potterhanworth, Lincolnshire
Printed in Great Britain by Ashford Colour Press, Gosport, Hampshire

*Inter-Varsity Press publishes Christian books that are true to the Bible and that
communicate the gospel, develop discipleship and strengthen the church for its mission in
the world.*

*Inter-Varsity Press is closely linked with the Universities and Colleges Christian Fellowship,
a student movement connecting Christian Unions in universities and colleges throughout
Great Britain, and a member movement of the International Fellowship of Evangelical
Students. Website: www.uccf.org.uk*

Contents

Acknowledgments

Big thanks to all who've helped me with this book in lots of different ways – you know who you are!

This book is dedicated with love to my children, Joshua, Samuel and bump, and to my godchildren, David, Abigail and Rachel. Remember: just because I'm a vicar doesn't make me a Christian. And just because *I'm* a Christian doesn't make *you* a Christian.

Foreword

I'm a Christian, aren't I? is not written to be read in one sitting, but I couldn't put it down.

Maybe it was the subject matter that I found appealing. It strikes me that it is possible to go through life and get things wrong about most things. But to have mistaken who is the real Jesus, and what he said about Christianity, is too great an error. If Jesus' words are to be believed, then that has eternal consequences. Dan Clark explains from the Bible who Jesus is, and clearly he is not the BBC Jesus, or even the RE lesson Jesus.

Perhaps Dan's logical presentation of what it really means to be a Christian is what held my attention. Step by step, he builds a case that is straightforward to follow, and makes so much sense. Dan takes his arguments directly from the Bible, rather than imposing his interpretations on the text. In so doing, the Bible comes to life. The Christian message is penetratingly clear, and left me wondering how it is that so many people just miss the point.

As I read on, I found myself anticipating the real-life stories of people being confronted with the Christian faith, some coming to God in a life-transforming way. Again, it all seemed anchored in what Jesus taught, as well as the realities of life.

The people Dan has met, and the questions they ask, are just like the friends I have, and the issues with which some of them struggle. Dan is an ordinary vicar, working in a thriving parish church, writing about the extraordinary God who is working today in the lives of all types of men and women. To miss out on this is the greatest tragedy. Dan explains why as he puts the pieces of Christian experience together.

What he says is too important to neglect.

Roger Carswell

Introduction:
Unwrapping the jigsaw puzzle

Which of these people would you call a Christian?

Frank has been a keen member of his local church for years. But when he tells his colleagues at work that he's a Christian, they give each other knowing looks. Frank is known as a really mean boss who doesn't keep his word, and who demands people work long hours whilst he knocks off early.

Ben has just arrived at university. He's been going to church up until now, and considers himself a Christian and pretty moral. But his priorities for the next three years are making friends and partying hard – he's not planning to let religion get in the way of that.

Jill has two kids. She's also a foster mum, and is considering adopting a baby from China. She's always holding charity fund-raising events in her home, and she knows the names of most of the homeless people in the area – she helps on a soup run each week. She doesn't make a song and dance about helping others – she just does it.

Sasha started to go to church after her brother was killed in a car crash. She's grown to really appreciate the peace and stability church gives her – and the great friends. But she's never really got all the God-talk they do. She joins in everything, and tries to live a good life, but deep down she suspects the Jesus thing is all made up.

Some would say that Frank is a Christian because he goes to church. Others would say he isn't, because he clearly doesn't lead a very Christian life.

Some would say Ben is a Christian because he has a church background and is a moral person. Others would say he isn't, because it's not his current priority.

Some of Jill's friends would say she's the most Christian person they know – she leads such a wonderfully selfless life. Others admire her good works, but would say she's not a Christian because she doesn't go to church.

Sasha's friends are sure she's a Christian, but Sasha's not so sure.

It's not always easy to work out who is and who isn't a Christian.

When I tell people I'm a vicar, most people change the subject straightaway. Occasionally people tell me I'm far too young to be a vicar (although that's happening less now, sadly). Sometimes people launch into their understanding of Christianity:

- 'I'm a Christian – I try to lead a good life.'
- 'I was christened as a baby – that makes me a Christian, doesn't it?'
- 'Christians believe in God, don't they? I believe in aliens.'
- 'I'm Church of England. I love to go at Christmas.'
- 'I was born here, so I suppose I'm a Christian.'
- 'I was born again at a Billy Graham rally forty years ago.'

It seems there are many different ideas about what it means to be a Christian. What would you say a Christian is?

Real lives – Gloria

Throughout this book, I'll get some friends of mine to tell their stories. Gloria, in her mid-fifties, is a retired primary school teaching assistant and a keen runner.

I was one of seven children, brought up as a Roman Catholic by an English father and an Italian mother. For me, going to Mass was neither inspirational nor interesting, especially as half of it was in Latin! Sunday school was much the same. I was raised to be seen and not heard, so we didn't ask questions. There was much I didn't understand and I grew up in the fear of God. I had lots of negative thoughts about the Catholic faith so, when I was old enough to choose, I stopped going to church and never went back. I have tried since then to live a good and moral life, but I have always felt there was something missing.

One day last year, I got talking to a Christian friend about my experience with religion. He suggested I went to church with him. It wasn't life changing, but I soon heard about a course called Christianity Explored and thought it would be good for me.

After each session I attended, it became more and more clear I had got God all wrong! By the end of the course, I had changed my whole understanding of what it means to be a Christian. I used to think that God was judgmental, which made me feel somehow unworthy of his love. Now I feel so much more at ease and secure in my relationship with God, because I know he loves me unconditionally.

There is still so much to know and I am slowly trying to change some 'unchristian' habits I've acquired through the years – but it's so much easier knowing God is on my side, helping and guiding me. It all makes so much more sense to me now – all I had to do was pray!

Let me be clear: I'm not asking what makes someone a Christian simply out of intellectual curiosity. In my experience, when people who think of themselves as Christians have a less-than-clear understanding of what a Christian is, they often have a less-than-satisfying experience of being a Christian. Let me give you three examples.

1. Those who are confused

When someone says to me, 'I think I'm a Christian' or 'I'm a sort-of Christian' or 'I ticked the "Christian" box on the census form, because I knew I wasn't any of the others', I always feel saddened – because God wants us to have *confidence* when it comes to our understanding of God and our relationship with him. Not that we'll ever have God all summed up (how arrogant would that be!), or never have doubts (every Christian doubts at times). But we should have a quiet assurance that God knows us and loves us.

Do you have an assurance that God knows you and loves you, or are there elements of confusion about your faith, or your relationship with God? If so, I hope that this book will help to bring you clarity and confidence with God.

2. Those who are disappointed with God

Jen is in her twenties. Her big secret is that she had an abortion eight years ago. A friend recently became a Christian and talks incessantly about having her sins forgiven and knowing God's peace. She can't see how God could forgive her, when she can't even forgive herself . . .

Bill is in his forties, and has gone to church since he got married – reluctantly at first, but now he quietly enjoys it. Over a beer, some guys from church talk about God guiding them. Bill could do with some guidance right now, but has never felt God's guidance in his life.

Mary is in her seventies. She started coming back to church after her husband died ten years ago. She's had a heart attack recently, and knows she won't live many more years. She'd love to think she was going to heaven, but doesn't know how she can be sure.

All these people – and many like them – are disappointed. They thought that being a Christian would help them, but just when they really need help, it's not working. To put it another way, they want more from their Christian life. The good news of Christianity is that God really does want to give us more!

- Many feel weighed down by guilt at their past mistakes, yet God wants Christians to be sure *beyond doubt* that they are forgiven.
- Many wander aimlessly, uncertain what to do, yet God wants to give us his guidance and direction through life.
- Many fear death as a great unknown, yet God wants Christians to be confident that an infinitely better life awaits them beyond the grave.
- To many, God seems vague and distant, yet God wants Christians to know him as a friend.
- To many, prayer feels like talking to a brick wall, yet God wants Christians to be able to speak with him personally in prayer.

If you're the sort of person who is secretly or openly disappointed with God, and longs for more from your Christian life, I hope that this book will help your quest. The more we understand God's vision of what being a Christian can be, the more we'll grow in confidence with God, appreciating the richness of what it means to be his follower.

3. Those who stop short

A few years ago, my wife and I needed some travel insurance. I got various quotes – and then thought to check whether our credit card account already included travel insurance. When I looked carefully at the terms and conditions, I discovered all sorts of benefits that we'd been missing out on: money off car and home insurance, discounted entry to various tourist attractions, loyalty points at numerous shops – and free travel insurance.

I'd thought that a credit card was just a convenient way to pay for goods. In reality, it could have been so much more. I'd unwittingly stopped short of getting full benefit from the account.

I talk to lots of people who think of themselves as Christians – friends, neighbours, people who go to the church where I work. Sadly, I fear many of them are stopping short in their experience of the Christian life. They haven't appreciated just how wonderful life with God could be.

- Many think of God's rules as restrictive, yet Jesus said he came to bring 'life to the full'.[1]
- Many struggle with the same old weaknesses year after year, yet God wants to transform Christians for the better.
- To many, the Bible seems foreign, yet God wants to give Christians confidence in his promises.
- Many feel only a sense of duty and obligation towards God, yet God wants Christians to experience a unique freedom and deep-seated joy – that helps us even through dark times.
- Many find church tedious, yet God wants Christians to experience deeply loving friendships in a church.

If you can recognize yourself a bit in one of the portraits above, I hope this book will help you discover some 'member benefits' that you haven't yet realized exist!

The authentic Christian

I want to suggest that many people's struggles with the Christian life are simply because they have an incomplete picture of what an authentic Christian really is. If only we could get a complete picture, then much confusion about the Christian life would be cleared up, disappointments about the Christian life would be turned round, and many benefits of the Christian life would be realized.

Now, the last thing I want to do is give you *my* definition of a Christian, for that will be just as defective as anyone else's. My aim in this book is to look at *Jesus'* understanding of a Christian. Surely it's his perspective that matters? After all, if a *Christian* is a follower of Jesus *Christ*, doesn't he have the final say in the matter?

A few years ago, I parked my car in a street that I thought was a pay and display area. I bought a ticket, stuck it in the car, and went off to do my shopping. When I got back, I'd been slapped with a parking fine. It turns out the street was in a residents-only zone – and I didn't have a permit.

Of course, *my* definition of legal parking was somewhat irrelevant seeing as the *council* set the boundaries. Similarly, when it comes to defining a Christian, it doesn't really matter if *I* call myself a Christian. But what matters enormously is whether *Jesus* calls me a Christian.

Real lives – Dan

Dan, twenty-one, is a student and sci-fi fan.

I have always considered myself a Christian, based on my

parents' faith and the fact that the majority of people I knew were from the church. It wasn't until I started going along to a summer camp that I began to realize that there was more to faith in God than just 'being' a Christian. Eventually, I realized that if I was serious about being a Christian, I had to have my own faith – looking to Christ for my salvation – rather than simply assuming that I was a Christian because I had been brought up and lived in a certain way.

It didn't radically change the way I live, but it changed the way I thought about it. I now behaved as I did, not out of a sense of duty or religious necessity, but out of love and respect for the God who created and saved me.

Let the puzzle begin

I hope I've begun to raise a few questions in your mind, and to whet your appetite. To describe Jesus' understanding of what it means to follow him, I'm going to adopt a simple jigsaw puzzle. It has only five pieces. The challenge won't be to put the pieces together; the challenge will be to make sure *all* the pieces are present. The following chapters will look at each jigsaw piece in turn – feel free to read them in whatever order you want, maybe starting with the jigsaw piece which most intrigues you, or about which you've got most questions.

It turns out that many of the popular definitions of a Christian I mentioned earlier have some truth to them: according to Jesus, a genuine Christian does *believe* in God and Jesus (and some other things!); they do *belong* to a local church; they do seek to *behave* – by living a good life; they have been *baptized*; they have been *born again*.

As we look at each piece of the jigsaw in turn, I hope you'll see that no single piece is a complete picture of what it means to be a Christian. In fact, even having two, three or four of the pieces is insufficient. It's only when all five pieces are in place that Jesus' picture of an authentic Christian emerges.

Remember, that's the real question: would Jesus call *me* a Christian? And would he call *you* a Christian?

Questions for reflection

At the end of each chapter, there are some questions for reflection, largely based on Jesus' teaching. Use a modern translation of the Bible.[2] *The questions can be done individually or in a group. If you're not used to reading the Bible for yourself, or are doubtful about the reliability of the Bible, you may find some of the books in the 'Further reading' section helpful.*

1. Do you think of yourself as a Christian? Why / why not?
2. If you do call yourself a Christian, what has been your experience of the Christian life – can you relate to feelings of being confused, or disappointed with God? Do you think there may be more 'member benefits' you haven't yet received?

   Turn to John 10, where Jesus famously said, 'I am the good shepherd' – and by implication, likens us to sheep.

3. Read verses 1–10, where Jesus contrasts himself with the thief or robber. Whose voice should we listen to? Why?
4. Read verses 11–18, where Jesus contrasts himself with a temping shepherd – the hired hand. Why should we trust Jesus rather than others? Can you say you know Jesus

(verse 14) in the very personal way Jesus indicates is possible?

5. Read verses 19–21, where Jesus' claims caused a divided response. As we go through this book, are you prepared to listen to Jesus and take his words seriously?

6. Glance back through this introduction. Talk to God in your own words about something that has challenged or encouraged you.

Piece 1: Believing

'I'm pretty sure there is a God, but I do have doubts. Some days they're bigger than others. For instance, there are those scientists who say they've disproved God. Even if there is a God, I don't like the way different religions all claim to be right – that's not very tolerant, is it? Maybe there's no way to find out for sure about God.' (Sanjay, thirty-two)

'Our church says the creed: "I believe in God . . . " Looking round, it seems as though some people say it with great conviction, but most sort of mumble through it, unsure what some words mean, and with little thought to what the implications might be. It's just a part of the ritual. I definitely believe in God. I'm not so sure Jesus was God, but I'm happy to call him a son of God.' (Issy, fifty-five)

A few weeks ago, an email I received mentioned a newspaper article headed 'Britons are believers of fuzzy faith, says survey'.[1]

Intrigued, I clicked on the link to read on. As it turns out, the description of someone with fuzzy faith fitted some of my friends: someone whose idea of God is rather vague, and whose relationship to any church is quite weak. Of course, many of these people would still describe themselves as 'spiritual' and 'moral' – but they might prefer to talk about a 'Higher Power' than about 'God', and they don't like to take the whole package of religion on board.

Maybe that's how you'd describe yourself.

There are lots of different reasons why people might describe their faith as fuzzy:

- I've met teenagers and young adults who tell me that they went to church schools, but 'weren't really interested' in the religious side of things.
- Other people have told me they used to believe, but then life got in the way – they encountered tragedy or terrible suffering, which has poured cold water over the fire of faith, reducing it to smouldering ashes.
- I've met young couples who've been overwhelmed at the birth of their children, and it's made them realize that 'there must be something out there'.
- A few people have told me that they've been attending church for years, but have never really understood the language used in church – so their belief in God is still quite vague.
- Some older people gave up going to church years ago, but have never fully abandoned a belief in God.
- I've met still others who think that 'science has all the answers now', leaving them with a much-reduced faith in God.[2]

I have a lot of sympathy for such people, and respect their honesty. Many people's faith seems to rise and fall at different points in their lives. For me, it was being awed by the beauty and grandeur of creation that helped set me on the road to faith. I can remember being blown away by the sheer majesty of a mountain range, and being speechless as I watched the incredible colours of a sunset.

But is it possible to progress from a fuzzy faith? Can we know with any greater certainty what God is like? As someone said, 'If there is a God, why doesn't he just send someone down?'

In fact, that's exactly what God has done!

Getting God in focus

I'd love to be a great photographer – although I'm not sure I've got the patience to become one! Our camera is pretty basic, but on occasion, I'm able to borrow the sort of camera where, as you look through the viewfinder and adjust the lens, suddenly the subject comes into focus.

When Jesus stepped into our world, he was bringing God into focus. As we look at the birth, life, death and resurrection of Jesus of Nazareth, our picture of God can stop being fuzzy and become sharply focused. As we read the pages of the Gospels, we can watch how he interacts with the good and the godless, listen to him speak, see what motivates him, and sense the awe that he generated. Jesus spoke of God as 'the Father who sent him'[3] – and he said, 'Anyone who has seen me has seen the Father.'[4] His point is clear: as we look at Jesus, we see God himself.

The implication of this is that God doesn't intend for us to have a fuzzy faith. If Jesus has come into our world to show us what God is like, he wants us to have a focused picture of him. So what is God like?

A million miles away or down to earth?
Most people who work for huge multinational companies never get to meet the Managing Director. Employees might respect him (or her) for leading such a large, successful company. And depending on the culture of the company, they might even fear the MD, and not feel able to say anything bad about the company. But they almost certainly wouldn't know the MD, nor expect the MD to know them.

Some people relate to God in much the same way: they would say that they respect him, maybe even fear him. But they don't know him, and wouldn't expect him to know them – after all, they operate in different spheres. To them, God is a distant being. Is that how you think about God?

It turns out that we don't need to look a million miles away for God; he's walked this earth. And in Jesus, he's experienced every aspect of our human lives. In fact, he's experienced more injustice and suffering than most people (at least in the West) will ever do. He was born in the equivalent of a farmyard barn – not in a royal palace or private hospital, as might have been befitting for the king of the universe. As a toddler, his family was forced to flee from tyrannical infanticide (targeted at Jesus), becoming refugees in a foreign country. When he became a travelling preacher, it seems that he was extremely poor, and probably homeless. He frequently encountered opposition from powerful religious authorities, who tried to silence him. Jesus was betrayed by one of his followers, and abandoned by all his close friends. His trial was almost certainly illegal and stocked with false witnesses. His death sentence was confirmed by a spineless politician who was convinced of Jesus' innocence – yet who bowed to public pressure. He died a criminal's death, hanging from a cross in the searing Middle Eastern heat, naked and humiliated, gasping for breath.

It is just extraordinary that God should *choose* to experience human life in all its pain and vulnerability like this. Jesus shatters the notion that God is remote and uninterested in human life. We don't need to relate to him as to a distant MD, because he doesn't want to relate to us like that.

Abstract or personal?

Darth Vader said to Luke Skywalker, 'I know what you're getting for your birthday.'

'How come?' replied Luke.

'I felt your presence.'

Groan! Another common notion of God goes like this: he's a spiritual force (in true *Star Wars* style), an energy that runs and flows between all of us. In other words, God is a bit like electricity or microwaves: powerful and unseen. But imagine being told to 'love electricity' – you can't love an impersonal thing! Yet Jesus said that the most important commandment is to 'love the Lord your God with all your heart and with all your soul and with all your mind'.[5] Do you see? Jesus assumes that God is not only powerful and unseen, but also very personal – and he says that the most important thing in the world is for us to love him. Not just to love the *idea* of God. But to love God *personally* with every ounce of our being.

Certainly, the Bible doesn't talk about 'God' as an abstract – as some theory to be believed in. Rather, it shows God as he deals personally with ordinary humans like you and me. 'I am the bread of life,' Jesus said. 'Whoever comes to me will never go hungry, and whoever believes in me will never be thirsty.'[6] Jesus was saying that he hadn't come just to lay down a new philosophy, but to *satisfy* those who are hungry and thirsty for meaning in life. Similarly, when Jesus said, 'I am the light of the world. Whoever follows me will never walk in darkness, but will have the light of life',[7] he was saying that he hadn't come just to lay down a new list of rules, but to help *guide* those who walk somewhat aimlessly through life so that they can find the 'light of life'.

Since God is a personal God, a vitally important question emerges: do we know God personally?

If I were to read the autobiography of my favourite footballer, I'd know a lot about him, but it wouldn't mean we were friends with each other. We wouldn't talk on the phone; he wouldn't text me from his latest luxury holiday.

Can you say that you *know* God, or do you feel that you might only know things *about* God? Can you say that you *love* God?

Real lives – Liz

Liz, twenty-seven, is a full-time mother who likes scrapbooking.

I went to church with my parents as a child. It was just a thing that we did on a Sunday. It was quite boring, and when I started my GCSEs I just stopped going.

After I went to university, my partner and I were told it would be hard for us to have children, yet everyone around us seemed to be getting pregnant. In one desperate moment, crying, I prayed – for the first time truthfully and believing in God – that he would grant us the opportunity to have a baby. Three months later I discovered I was pregnant!

After getting married and having our son, I started to think that I wanted my son to go to church as I had. A couple of weeks later I started to attend a Christianity Explored course, mainly because I was interested in the crèche and in making friends. But that very first meeting and talking with other Christians got me thinking: what if there is something more in this than I realize, and it isn't just about believing in 'something'? The penny-dropping moment for me was when we were talking about grace, and I realized that God sent his Son to die and take away our sins, and that we are saved by his grace.

I'm learning that God works in every aspect of our lives, and that trusting in him is the way we should live.

The Bishop of Durham, Tom Wright, wrote:

Christian spirituality combines a sense of the awe and majesty of God with a sense of his intimate presence . . . As Jesus addresses God as 'Father', so Christians are encouraged to do the same, to come to know God in the way in which, in the best sort of family, the child knows the parent. From time to time I have met churchgoers who look puzzled at this, and say that they have no idea what all that stuff is about. I have to say that being a Christian without something at least of that intimate knowledge of the God who is at the same time majestic, awesome and holy sounds to me like a contradiction in terms.[8]

Could that be describing you? God wants us to know him personally, and if that sense of 'intimate presence' is lacking, then it may be a sign that the 'believing' piece of the jigsaw is missing or at least sadly misshaped.

Indifferent or compassionate?

It can be illuminating to ask people who don't believe in God, 'What sort of God don't you believe in?' Almost invariably, they have quite a clear picture of the god-they-don't-believe-in. So when they say they don't believe in God, they often mean they don't believe in a God who is authoritarian, harsh, judgmental and uncaring.

The great news is, that's not the sort of God Christians believe in, either.

A quick glance through the Gospels shows that Jesus was anything but indifferent as he met human need face to face. Several times, we read that Jesus was full of compassion – a deep, stomach-churning desire to help people. On one occasion, we read that Jesus was moved to tears.

Throughout his ministry, he demonstrated an intense concern for individuals. When a blind man tried to call out to Jesus, only to be silenced by the crowds, Jesus summoned him and healed him. When a woman, set up and humiliated by 'holier than thou' religious officials, was brought to Jesus in fear of her life, he turned the judgment instead on her accusers, and granted her pardon. When young children clamoured to see Jesus, only to be turned away by his over-officious disciples, Jesus welcomed them and blessed them. When a man was scared to be seen speaking to Jesus, they met instead under cover of darkness. When an unpopular, money-grabbing civil servant shinned up a tree to catch sight of Jesus, Jesus chose to spend time with him, turning his life around.

All this points us to the conclusion that God is concerned about *us, our* life, *our* struggles, *our* needs. Jesus called people by name, as he calls you by name. Imagine: the powerful God of the universe, taking a personal interest in you!

Perfect, or just powerful?
I read a novel recently about the owner of a chemical company that had polluted local water supplies, leading to many cancer

deaths. The billionaire owner used his money to buy a legal victory, even though the evidence was stacked against him. It's often been said that 'Power corrupts and absolute power corrupts absolutely.'

But how about God? If he's got absolute power, has it corrupted him? Can he be trusted?

One of the things I find most unnerving in the Gospels is the sheer quality of Jesus' life. Jesus said, 'Your heavenly Father is perfect.'⁹ Significantly, Jesus' friends said the same thing about him. Having lived alongside him for three years, they concluded, 'He committed no sin, and no deceit was found in his mouth.'¹⁰

Think of something completely pure: a freshly painted wall, with no blemishes; a ski slope at dawn after a fresh snowfall; a clear blue Mediterranean sky with not a cloud in sight. That is a picture of Jesus' moral perfection.

If we're honest, that stands in stark contrast to us. However hard we try, we let ourselves and others down – even by our own standards. When we consider God's standards, we realize our failings even more. Think: have you never lied (even a little white lie)? Have you never stolen anything (even a phone call from your office phone line)? Have you never sworn by God's or Jesus' name? Have you always honoured your parents? Have you never wished you had something belonging to someone else (their car/looks/children/garden, etc.)? That's half of the Ten Commandments broken already! But that is merely a *symptom* of a deeper problem within us: the fact that we haven't loved God with all our heart, soul, mind and strength, as he's asked us to. All of our individual sins are actually a consequence of a failure to love God.

Think of a white wall with a toddler's pen drawings on; a ski slope so heavily used that it's turned to dirty slush; a sky with grey cloud and heavy rain moving towards you. That is a picture of our moral imperfection.

So, whilst Jesus turns out to be perfectly powerful and powerfully perfect, we turn out to be neither powerful nor perfect. The Bible makes it clear that, although God made us humans to be in personal friendship with him, our sin now blocks that friendship. That's one of the reasons why many people complain, 'I pray to God. But it feels like praying to a brick wall. I never get an answer.' The problem is that there is something between us and God – not a wall, but our sin.

Condemning or rescuing?

When I do weddings, I occasionally find that some people are very hesitant about coming into the church building, because they half expect a lightning bolt from heaven to strike them down! They know that they haven't even attempted to live as God wants them to live most of the time, making them almost frightened about stepping into 'God's house'.

I'm pleased to say that no-one's yet been struck by lightning when they come in! But their nervousness shows that their mental picture of God is of someone who's out to get them. In fact, nothing could be further from the truth. The name 'Jesus' means 'God saves' or 'God rescues' – and that indicates that, above all, Jesus didn't just come to bring our picture of God into sharp focus; he came to rescue us.

At the end of the day, every religion offers some link between people and their god – a kind of ladder. But religions are like wooden ladders: they involve humans climbing up from the ground, attempting to reach whatever particular goal (Paradise, Nirvana, etc.) is on offer. Many people assume that Christianity works in the same way. As a student said to me the other day,

'What do I have to do to make sure God is happy with me and that I'm a Christian?'

The good news is that the Christian faith is actually quite different from other religions in two ways. First, it's a *rope* ladder, let down from heaven to us, not a wooden ladder reaching up from the ground. Second, it's *Jesus* who does the climbing, not us! As the Christmas carol says, 'He came down to earth from heaven.' Why? To rescue us.

So God isn't out to condemn us. Jesus himself said, he 'came to look for and to save people'.[11] It's a completely free rescue service! We don't have to earn God's favour, merely receive it. It takes no effort on our part – having come down the ladder to rescue us, it's as though he then gives us a fireman's lift back up the ladder. We can just enjoy the ride!

As a Christian, I know that I can't rescue myself – I'll never be good enough for God. When I start climbing up the ladder towards God, I'll soon slip down a few rungs as I disobey him or disregard him. But I take comfort from the fact that Jesus himself described his death as 'a ransom for many'[12] – indicating that his death would be a sacrifice from which many people could benefit – including me and you.

One evening I made the mistake of pouring chicken fat down the kitchen sink. Never again. You can guess what happened – the drains blocked, so the following morning I was lying on the ground outside with my arm down the drain, trying to clear the mess. It was a horrible job (you can imagine what else was down there!) – but talk about job satisfaction! As soon as the last bit of the obstruction was gone, the water from the sink drained away in no time at all – the drains could work as they were meant to work.

Jesus said that he came to save us, but the flip side to his message was that we must 'repent'. That is, we must turn back to God in sorrow for our sins. It's easy to think of repentance as a negative thing – like going through all the mess in the drain to clear the blockage. But actually, it's a really positive thing, because when the obstacle is gone, our relationship with God is restored – we can live as we were meant to live.

We've all offended people on occasion – sometimes deliberately, sometimes accidentally. Of course, for a friendship to be restored, it needs both parties to make up. One must say 'sorry', the other must forgive. When it comes to mending our relationship with God, Jesus has already made the first move – he's offered us God's forgiveness by his death on the cross; but we must respond with repentance. Otherwise, the relationship remains broken.

Imagine you develop blood poisoning. It's a potentially fatal condition, but relatively easy to cure with antibiotics if diagnosed early enough. What must you do? Believing *that* the antibiotics can cure you isn't enough! You must *take* the antibiotics in order to be cured.

So it is with God – he wants to save us (and Jesus has died in order to save us), but we must take the cure, letting him save us. Do you believe that God can forgive sins – and if so, have you asked him to save you from *your* sins?

Beginning to believe

So far, we've seen that God doesn't want us to have a vague picture of what he's like, but a clearly focused picture. As we look at Jesus, we see that God is reaching out to us with great compassion, wanting not to condemn us, but to rescue us. I think it's a wonderful picture! Don't you?And as our picture of God becomes clearer, it means our response to God can become firmer. Our faith doesn't need to be fuzzy.

Professor Alister McGrath wrote:

> A surprising number of people who think of themselves
> as Christians never get further than accepting the truth of
> Christianity. They believe that God is there – but they have never
> met him. They believe that God is able to forgive sins – but they
> have never allowed God to forgive *their* sins. They believe that
> God is reliable – but they have never relied upon him. People
> like this were called 'half-way' believers in eighteenth-century
> America. They are on their way to faith – but they have yet to
> arrive. The richness and depth of the gospel remains something
> unknown to them.[13]

Maybe you're in that position: half-way to belief. Many people
who grew up with Christianity – at home or at school – only
ever get half-way to belief. To put it another way, it's only got
as far as their heads, and hasn't sunk down to their hearts.

Or to change the analogy again, it may be helpful to
think of 'belief' having two layers, the second building on the
first:

1. *'I believe' means 'I am of the opinion that'*. For example, to
   say 'I believe in ghosts' affirms a belief in the existence of
   ghosts.
2. *'I believe' means 'I trust' or 'I have confidence in'*. For
   example, we might 'trust a surgeon' to operate on us.

Christian belief in God involves both levels. It is a belief *that*
God exists, but more importantly, it's deciding to *trust* in
that God. To trust in God means that we willingly rely on him
and follow his leading; we allow him to challenge us and rule
over us; we allow him to save us.

Real lives - Ian

Ian, thirty-six, is a currently unemployed snowboard enthusiast.

I was born into a church family. As a young man I professed a faith, but looking back I realized it was more like my parents' faith for me rather than my own. At university, I dropped out of church and Christian life completely. I just enjoyed myself in the party scene instead.

In my mid-twenties, I moved to New York with work. After a while I started living with a girl. As the relationship went on, I became increasingly lonely, isolated and tired. More and more, I felt something in my life was missing, so I started going to church again. At first I went on my own, and started to get some peace. I began to realize where I should be. Then, after a while, my girlfriend started coming with me because she wanted to see what I was so interested in. Initially she began light-hearted mickey-taking, but then it got nasty.

At this point I was lost; I didn't know what to do because I liked the girl, but she didn't want me to go to church. This was the first time I truly prayed out in despair. It became a straight choice between her and God.

God won. For the first time in my life I made a stand, a profession of faith, and gave everything to the Lord. Becoming a Christian was a growing process for me, one that started when I was a child. But it wasn't until that day when I was forced to make a choice that I truly felt like a Christian.

If you're only half-way to belief, I wonder what's stopping you going further?

- Maybe you're afraid that God is not interested in *you*. But as we look at Jesus and see God, there's ample evidence of his compassion and concern for everyone: male and female, young and old, rich and poor, popular and despised, good and bad.
- Maybe you feel that he wouldn't accept the likes of you – that you're not good enough for him – but remember, none of us are good enough for him. Yet Jesus promised that 'Whoever comes to me I will never drive away.'[14]
- Maybe you're afraid of trusting in God – letting him shape your decisions and actions. You're afraid that it would take the fun out of life! But Jesus said, 'I have come that they may have life, and have it to the full'[15] – and countless genuine Christians around the world, including me, will happily tell you that, although trusting God might be scary at times, it's the way to find genuine fullness of life. Besides, if Jesus has already demonstrated his love and concern for us by laying down his life for us, can we really not trust him?

In his earthly ministry, Jesus constantly urged people to 'believe' in him, and in his message and ministry. For example, when asked 'What must we do to do the works God requires?' Jesus answered, 'The work of God is this: to *believe* in the one he has sent.'[16] (Imagine *me* telling you that all that God requires from your life is that you believe in *me* – it's laughable! Yet Jesus was quite serious about it.)

Again, Jesus talked about belief in him bringing eternal life and salvation: 'For God so loved the world that he gave his one

and only Son, that whoever *believes* in him shall not perish but
have eternal life.'[17] But that promise was followed by a stark
warning about the fate of those who fail to believe in him:
'Whoever believes in him is not condemned, but whoever *does
not believe* stands condemned already because he has not believed
in the name of God's one and only Son.'[18]

Jesus' call hasn't changed. He doesn't ask people today to
respect him as a great teacher or hail him as a spiritual guru.
Instead, he encourages people – me and you – to trust him as
God. Do you trust him? It's only as we trust him that we discover
his peace, his cleansing from guilt, his guidance, his transforming power – in short, the life that we were made to live. The
Gospels aren't written so that we can know *about* Jesus. They
were 'written that you may believe that Jesus is the Messiah, the
Son of God, and that by believing you may have life in his name'.[19]

Is belief enough?

But what if you already trust in Jesus? That is, what if both layers
of belief in God (i.e. believing that God exists and having
confidence that God saves us) are already in place? Such belief
is one vital piece of the jigsaw – but it turns out it's not the *only*
piece. In fact, the Bible is quite blunt: 'Faith by itself, if it is not
accompanied by action, is dead.'[20] Our faith has to be worked
out in practice in many different areas of our lives. We need to
look at another piece of the jigsaw.

Questions for reflection

1. Imagine you're asked to write a character reference for
   God. What would you write? What evidence could you
   give?

Turn to Mark 1, the introduction to what was probably the first Gospel to be written.

2. Read verses 1–13. Who does Mark think Jesus is? Who or what backs up his claim?
3. Read verses 14–15. How does Jesus announce his arrival? What do you find surprising about that? What response does Jesus look for?
4. Read verses 16–20. In what ways did these ordinary people trust Jesus? When did you last trust Jesus? How?
5. Read verses 21–28. How do these verses show us Jesus as an involved God, a personal God and a saving God? What examples could you give from your own life?
6. Glance back through the chapter. Talk to God in your own words about something that's challenged or encouraged you.

Piece 2: Belonging

'When I was at school, we had this awful end-of-year church service. The vicar wore a dress, the choir sang something in Latin, the readings were incomprehensible . . . we'd while away the time looking at magazines we'd smuggled in.' (JD, twenty-two)

'I went to Sunday school for a few years as a child. When my own children were in the Scouts, I went with them to church. Harvest and Christmas were good – but all the rituals and dogma kill it off the rest of the year. I prefer to be at home: you can pray in the garden, but you can't do the gardening in church.' (Janet, forty-six)

A father was showing his daughter around a church building, when he pointed out the war memorial. 'Those are the names of those who died in the services,' the dad explained. 'Which services were they?' the girl asked. 'Morning or evening?'

Church has been described as 'the most boring experience on offer'. I've certainly been to some church services where I've thought, 'What was the point of that?' But I've been to many more where I've come away feeling energized and challenged.

Many people's experience of church is of being forced to attend Sunday school or of going to funerals. And let's face it, no child enjoys anything they're forced to do and no adult enjoys funerals. Even in regular Sunday services, all too often the songs are unknown and unsingable; the sermon uses unfamiliar language and seems irrelevant; the coffee is disgusting and tepid; the seats are hard and uncomfortable. No wonder that according to one recent report, although 26 million people in the UK consider themselves 'Christian', less than one in three of these go to church at least once a month, and only half of them go to church at least once a year.[1]

What is church?

If I asked someone on the street to do a word association exercise on 'church', they might say things like 'cold, old building, spire, pews, stained-glass windows, candles'. That is, they would think about the *physical building* that we call 'a church'.

The Bible's definition is completely different. It says the church is the *people* who meet in Jesus' name, not the *place* where they meet. In fact, many churches meet in community centres, school halls, or – in some parts of the world – the open air. So a church is simply a gathering of Christians (although others are welcome to attend as well), which can happen anywhere (not just in an old building with pews, etc.) and at any time (not just on a Sunday).

And the Bible holds out an exciting vision of church as a group of people characterized by a deep concern for each other.

That's something many people in our culture actually desire, deep down. At a surface level, we're the most 'connected' generation our world has ever known – it's so easy to stay in touch with a wide variety of people via the web and texts. Yet many of these 'friendships' are fairly superficial.

Many people feel increasingly 'alone in a crowd', feeling that there's no-one who truly understands them for who they are, no-one who really knows what makes them tick. Maybe you sense that yourself.

The good news is that God hasn't created us to be alone. He's created us for connection, not isolation – and God has given us the church as the place for that to happen.

Picture postcards of the church

If you've been into beautiful church buildings, you've doubtless seen postcards of the buildings on sale. The Bible gives us various pictures of the church – but they're not photographs of the building. They're images taken from everyday life which have parallels in how a church (the people) works.

1. The church is the family of God

Some people, sadly, have *bad* experiences of family life. The church is likened to family life *at its best*. On one occasion, Jesus pointed to his followers, saying, 'Here are my mother and my brothers. For whoever does the will of my Father in heaven is my brother and sister and mother.'[2] In other words, Jesus viewed his motley collection of disciples – the people who lived and travelled with him, seeking to learn from, and be led by him – as his family.

That's not to say church families are perfect – far from it! The poor church family I'm part of have to put up with me, with all my weaknesses and foibles. Just as no-one chooses their physical brothers and sisters – meaning they don't always get on – so Christians don't choose their spiritual brothers and sisters, and that can cause problems. Jesus told his followers to 'love one another', giving himself as an example of what love should look like: 'As I have loved you, so you must love one another.'[3] The apostle Paul wrote, 'Let us do good to all people, especially to those who belong to the family of believers.'[4]

It's a tremendous privilege to be on the receiving end of that love. In church, I find a depth of friendship that I don't find anywhere else. It's so wonderful to have a group of people who are genuinely concerned for my welfare. When our children had just been born, people at church brought round meals to help us through the first few chaotic weeks. When we moved to a new part of the country, we were quickly welcomed into our new church so that we soon started to feel that we 'belonged', rather than feeling alone and lost in a new place.

2. The church is like a building

Over the last few months, a building round the corner from us has been completely renovated. The old building was demolished; fresh foundations were dug; a new frame of steel girders was put in place; the walls have been built. We haven't appreciated the noise and disruption, but our two-year-old has loved the succession of diggers, cranes and dump-trucks!

The Bible says that although 'the church' isn't a *physical* building, it can be thought of as a *spiritual* building, with people as bricks. Writing to a group of Christians, the apostle Paul says, 'You are like a building with the apostles and prophets as the foundation and with Christ as the most important stone. Christ is the one who holds the building together and makes it grow into a holy temple for the Lord. And you are part of that building Christ has built.'[5]

We learn several things from this picture:

- The teaching we find in the Bible (the writings of the apostles and prophets) is the foundation of the church – take the Bible away, and the church would soon collapse!
- Jesus is 'the most important stone' (e.g. the stone holding an arch together, or girders providing a frame for a building) – in other words, it's not the vicar/pastor/priest/ minister who holds the church together – it's Jesus himself. He's also like the brick-layer, making the building grow.
- Individual Christians are a vital part of the building, too, like bricks. We're not left in a pile at the bottom, discarded and unused – but built together into walls.

So in any church, the Bible must clearly guide what is going on, Jesus must be the one who's exalted, and individual Christians must be actively involved. I hate it when people in our church says 'You're much more important than me – you're the vicar!' On the contrary, I'm just one brick in the wall, next to them. It's Jesus who's the important one, and it's him who's building them and me together.

What draws a church together isn't just friendship. The bonds are spiritual. A church is a group of people who each know the love of God the Father, who are united in their gratefulness for what Jesus has done for us, and who are open to the work of God's Spirit changing us as individuals and as a group together. It's this spiritual unity that transcends age, class and cultural divisions. In one church I belonged to, as well as people from the UK, we had people from many African countries, the West Indies, India, Pakistan, China, Japan, America, Australia,

Indonesia, Mexico, Israel, Germany . . . and on the list went. For me, it was a foretaste of heaven to feel deeply related to each of these people, from such differing backgrounds.

3. The church is the body of Christ

Think back to school human biology lessons, looking at the way our bodies are made up: different organs, bones, muscles, nerves and so on. So it is with the church: 'The body of Christ [the church] has many different parts, just as any other body does . . . A body isn't really a body, unless there is more than one part. It takes many parts to make a single body.'[6] It's as though when we look around any given church gathering, we see body parts strewn everywhere! – a leg, a hand, an eye, a mouth and so on. But together, those body parts make a whole body.

What's obvious when we think about our own bodies is that each part plays a vital different role, and no part by itself is sufficient. 'If our bodies were only an eye, we couldn't hear a thing. And if they were only an ear, we couldn't smell a thing. But God has put all parts of our body together in the way that he decided is best . . . the eyes cannot say they don't need the hands. That's also why the head cannot say it doesn't need the feet . . . Together you are the body of Christ. Each one of you is part of his body.'[7]

When I was at school, I loved being part of a 1930s style big band. It wasn't my favourite style of music, but it was where I learnt to be part of a team. Together, we played lots of gigs, made some albums and even got one or two mentions on the radio. There were some very good soloists in our number, but it was when we were all playing our unique parts that we sounded best.

The lessons from the body and the band are the same:

- Every Christian has a *unique* role to play in the church – how exciting!

- Every Christian has a *vital* role to play in the church – what status!
- No Christian *by themselves* is sufficient – what a relief!
- A whole church *together* represents Jesus where they live – what a challenge!

In the light of this teaching, John Stott, one of the most influential Christian leaders of the twentieth century, described 'unchurched Christians' as 'a grotesque anomaly', adding, 'the New Testament knows nothing of such a person'.[8] He's right. Just as you can't be in a band by yourself, you can't be a Christian by yourself. When we read of Jesus calling people in the Gospels, he told them to 'follow me', and join his growing band of disciples, rather than telling them to 'stay where you are by yourself'.

I was really encouraged recently to hear of a church where a lady who had been incredibly nervous and timid had come to the point where, with the encouragement of her church, she was able to lead the music from the front. Similarly, a man who was deaf and had been used to being on the fringe of church life, had been encouraged to make his unique contribution. He ended up writing songs for other deaf worshippers to sign together. That's a church that really recognizes each Christian as unique and vital.

Do I have to go to church to be a Christian?

Let's quickly review where we've got to. The church isn't a noun – something we *go to* – but a verb – something we *do* together. The church isn't a building, but the people. The church isn't made of stone, but of ordinary people who trust in Jesus. It's like a family (characterized by love), a building (being built by God) and a body (where each part plays a unique and vital role).

Note how each of these pictures have relationships at their heart – God hasn't made us for isolation, but for connectedness.

One recent survey got lots of non-churchgoers to visit a church to assess what it was like – a bit like mystery shoppers do for shops. Around 90% said the church they visited had a tangible sense of community. 'We thought it was going to be a hard slog,' said one couple involved in the research, 'but it wasn't at all. We loved it – and are thinking of going back.' In fact, over three-quarters of the visitors said they'd go back.[9]

Now, if someone is a Christian, yet *doesn't* go to church, what are the implications? We could picture a family gathering, where one sibling is missing – not because they've died or are on holiday; simply because they've chosen not to come. How sad for everyone else! Or we could picture a building where there are some gaps in the wall, and bricks left lying on the ground. The whole building is worse off – wind and rain can get in. Or we could picture a man confined to a wheelchair because his legs don't work. He might be good in a wheelchair, but it's harder work for the rest of his body, and it's not how the man was designed to be.

Each of those pictures is a sad parody of what it should be! In each case, the Christian who doesn't go to church makes the rest of the family/building/body much weaker. The whole body only 'grows and builds itself up in love *as each part does its work*'.[10] That's the experience of the bodybuilder: it's impossible to build your body up if one limb isn't joining in at all!

If we let our gaze turn to the 'missing piece' in these pictures, the story is even sadder. Whilst the family celebration goes on, picture a brother choosing to sit at home by himself. How insolent – and lonely! Picture a brick lying by itself in a building site – in danger of being kicked around or thrown into the skip. How vulnerable! Picture (if you have the stomach) a leg, amputated not because it was damaged beyond repair in a car accident, but simply because it decided it didn't want to be part of the rest of the body any more. How ridiculous!

These pictures reveal how Christians who don't play an active role in a local church miss out and even endanger themselves. For example:

- The Christian who divorces himself from his church family misses out on the great love and fellowship that the community wants to offer. God's purpose 'is not just to save isolated individuals and so perpetuate our loneliness, but rather to build his church'.[11] Just yesterday a fairly new Christian wrote to me, 'My [church] family have done so much for me; they have encouraged me, advised, explained and shared problems. I would not be where I am now without belonging to [this church].'
- The Christian who prefers to be a brick by themselves, rather than be part of the building, not only rejects the purpose for which they were created, but also misses out on the God-given means to spiritual blessing. For it's only as we let ourselves be 'built together' that we 'become a dwelling in which God lives by his Spirit'.[12]
- The Christian who chooses to be a limb cut off from the body has ultimately made a fatal decision. To do so is to commit spiritual suicide – the limb will quickly grow cold and die without blood pumping into it. Just as a wild lion will hunt a lone animal, rather than a pack, so the devil will more readily pounce on a lone Christian.[13]

No wonder one of the first church leaders said, 'Let us not give up meeting together, as some are in the habit of doing, but let us encourage one another.'[14]   Heb 10:25

Of course, most people who think it unnecessary to go to church to be a Christian are entirely unaware of the damage they do, both to the church (by not playing their part) and to themselves (by not receiving encouragement). Maybe some who are reading this count themselves in that number: you've never really stopped to think about why there are churches at all, instead of just individual Christians living out their individual Christian lives.

But as you've looked at these biblical pictures of a church, you've realized that 'going to church' is far more than just an optional extra for the Christian. It is part and parcel of what God has called us to. You should give it a go – and you could well be surprised. The mystery-shopper style survey of churches I mentioned earlier found that most churches made an effort to help newcomers understand and follow their services. One visitor added, 'I expected the sermon to make me feel guilty. It was a nice surprise to hear something relevant about current affairs.'

Rick Warren puts it this way: 'Most people think that Christianity is a *belief* system. There are beliefs in Christianity, but it's so much more. Christianity is a *belong* system.'[15]

Real lives – Amanda

Amanda, in her mid-fifties, is a special needs primary teacher.

Being a Christian has always been part of my life. I was baptized, confirmed and married in church, and it was important that my own children were baptized and confirmed and attended schools where they were exposed to regular worship.

However, for many years I had felt somewhat detached from my faith. I was irregular in my church attendance and prayed only very occasionally. When I did pray, I often included a prayer asking to be brought nearer to God and for a re-awakening of my faith. Two years ago, we attended a different church at Christmas, where I picked up some information about the Alpha course. I really enjoyed it and the follow-on course. The 'penny dropped' for me when I began to understand that faith is all about 'a relationship with God', and that was something that had totally passed me by over the years. It is that experience of a growing relationship with God, which spurs me on along this challenging journey that I feel I have begun. I've been surprised to feel more at peace with myself and more secure about the future.

I've also come to realize that you need the help and support of other Christians to keep you 'on the right track'. It is too hard to try to deepen your faith on your own, and weekly 'top-ups' are vital. Belonging to a home group is so helpful, as it provides that support and an insight into other people's everyday Christian lives. Without the support of others, I feel it would be all too easy to allow my faith to slip from the forefront of my mind or perhaps fade altogether.

I just wish I had started my journey a bit earlier in my life. I had the opportunity to, but just never really took it.

How can I get the most out of church?

Some people reading this will have had experiences of church that don't match up with these positive images. I asked one man recently, who'd grown up being very involved in a church, why he no longer went. 'I saw all the politics,' he said. 'It wasn't a nice place to be.' How tragic – when the church is supposed to be a family characterized by love. Other people have said how they went to a church for a while, but didn't feel valued or accepted. How awful – when the church is supposed to be a building where all Christians are 'a brick in the wall'.

Jesus himself made it clear that some churches are better than others – in one round of reports, he seemed to give only one church out of seven an 'A' grade.[16] But whilst there are no excuses for churches that don't exhibit love, teach faithfully and welcome new people in, the fact that some churches are poor is no excuse for Christians not to belong to a church.

John Stott puts the matter well:

> Some people construct a Christianity which consists entirely of a personal relationship to Jesus Christ and has virtually nothing to do with the church. Others make a grudging concession to the need for church membership, but add that they have given up the ecclesiastical institution as hopeless. Now it is understandable, even inevitable, that we are critical of many of the church's inherited structures and traditions. Every church in every place at every time is in need of reform and renewal. But we need to beware lest we despise the church of God . . . God has not abandoned his church, however displeased with it he may be . . . And if God has not abandoned it, how can we?[17]

If you're not currently playing an active part in a church, I wonder what is stopping you. It can be easy to make excuses – 'Sundays are my one chance for a lie-in'; 'My children have sports on a Sunday morning, and I want to support them'; 'If you saw my local church, you wouldn't go there either!' Some people find it genuinely scary to meet new people, or to go into an unfamiliar environment; others feel embarrassed about joining a church they've carefully avoided (or at least, kept at arm's length) for years.

But deep down, the issue is one of priority. If we truly recognize that to be a Christian involves not just belonging to *Christ*, but belonging to *his people*[18] as well (our new family!), then we will make membership of a church a priority, and re-order other parts of life around it.

I read the heart-warming story recently of two sisters who had been separated in World War II but were then reunited sixty-six years later. When the Japanese bombed Burma, they fled in opposite directions. One spent four months in refugee camps, before settling in Scotland. The other spent three years living under occupation, before fleeing to India. It was only when one of their daughters-in-law took up genealogy that the link was finally made. Now, they speak on the phone for three hours every Sunday!

If you describe yourself as a Christian but are not a regular part of a local church, you've got hundreds of long-lost brothers and sisters. Don't you want to find them and get to know them?

Some people may decide that rather than just complaining about a church from the fringes, they'll get involved to try to transform it from within. Others may be better off looking for a different church to the one they've experienced in the past – for although there are many bad churches around today, there are many good ones as well! The description of the very first church[19] suggests we ought to ask these sorts of questions when looking for a good church to be an active part of:

1. Does it teach from the Bible, showing how it applies to everyday life?

2. Does it have a deep and genuine fellowship, characterized by sacrificial love and an awareness of people's needs?
3. Is everyone encouraged to play their part?
4. Do they keep Jesus' sacrificial death central in their teaching and worship (for instance, in celebrating what different churches call 'Holy Communion', 'the Eucharist', 'the Lord's Supper' or 'Mass')?
5. Do they pray earnestly, seeking God's leading in everything they do, committing their plans to God in prayer?
6. Is there a sense of awe at God's presence with them and God's power among them?
7. Do they provide opportunities to meet in smaller groups as well as in a large gathering? (This is the best way to really belong, especially in a larger church.)
8. Do they sing God's praise in a heartfelt and enthusiastic way – not drearily?
9. Are they seen as a movement for good by the local community?
10. Do they encourage outsiders to put their trust in Jesus?

As with so many things in life, 'It is more blessed to give than to receive'[20] – the more we put into church (by using our God-given gifts and loving each other sacrificially), the more we will receive from church – and the more our appreciation of just how good God is will grow.

Real lives – Rich

Rich, twenty-one, is a student and part-time hospital porter.

When I arrived at secondary school, I was very surprised to be told I had to go to chapel three times a week, with hymn practice on Fridays. I was christened and confirmed, and went to some 'Prayer and Pizza' meetings with the vicar. But when I left school, I also left behind the Christian aspect of my life.

In my final year at university, a friend asked me to go on a Christianity Explored course with him. I agreed, even though I wasn't sure whether I really wanted to go. I enjoyed the first week and the people on my table were great, so I continued to go every week.

A major turning point was when I first had grace explained to me. I was amazed that we could be saved simply by putting our faith in Jesus Christ as Lord and Saviour, and that his death had the power to take away our sins, making us blameless in God's sight. This changed my whole perspective on what it meant to be a Christian, as nothing I do will change the extent of God's love for me.

Since rediscovering Christianity, I have been amazed at how welcoming and open everyone I meet at church and the various church events I go along to are. I really feel as though I have a great network of friends whom I can trust and go to when I need guidance. Previously I would have read a passage from the Bible, but not discussed it or applied its message to my life as a Christian. Now, with others, I have learnt to explore the Bible as never before.

I love having God in my life, seeking his guidance through the Bible and prayer. It's not always been easy, but I have a brighter outlook on life.

Is belonging to a church enough?

So far, we've seen that for a Christian to play an active part in a local church is 'taken as read' in the Bible. It's as 'two or three come together in my name' that Jesus promises, 'there am I with them'.[21] It's only our particularly individualistic Western culture that has allowed us even to think of being lone-ranger Christians!

But is belonging to a local church all there is to the Christian faith? Absolutely not! So what should we say to the person who thinks, 'I'm a Christian because I go to church'? Well, I've been to mosques, but that hasn't made me a Muslim. I've been to a Hindu temple, but that hasn't made me a Hindu. Similarly, we've had Jews come along to our church who wouldn't take kindly to being called Christians. Someone I know freely says that he went to church over a thousand times before he became a Christian!

More importantly, we have it from Jesus' own lips that the church will always include some 'imitation Christians' – people who *think* of themselves as Christians, and even persuade others that they're Christians, but whom *Jesus* won't recognize as his followers when he comes to judge us. And after all, it's *his* opinion that really matters. For example, when Jesus sent a message to a church in modern-day Turkey, he made it clear that not all of its members were genuine Christians.[22] As one writer comments, they were 'professing Christians who proved to be Christian in name only. They were tolerably respectable but nothing more. Their religious interest was shallow and casual.'[23]

In two parables, Jesus likened the 'kingdom of heaven' (a way of talking about the church) to a field with both wheat and weeds, and to a fisherman's net which contained both good fish and bad. At the end of both parables, a sorting took place:

the weeds were collected first and burned, before the wheat was harvested; and when the fishermen reached land, the good fish were kept whilst the bad fish were thrown away. In both parables, Jesus makes it clear that this sorting takes place 'at the end of the age' when 'the Son of Man [Jesus] will send out his angels, and they will weed out of his kingdom everything that causes sin and all who do evil'; or to put it another way, the angels 'will come and separate the wicked from the righteous'.[24]

J. K. Rowling's famous Harry Potter series pictures new students at Hogwarts School being allocated to one of the four school houses by a special 'Sorting Hat' which examines the pupil's mind. It determines who they live and study with for the entirety of their time at Hogwarts. That sorting is, of course, entirely fictional. The sorting that Jesus does at the end of time is very real and will determine our destination for the rest of eternity.

Now, *we* might not classify ourselves as 'wicked' or the kind of person who 'causes sin and does evil' – but the point is that *Jesus* says he'll find some of those people in the church. The lesson is clear: not all who think of themselves as Christians and belong to a church – not even all church leaders[25] – are genuine Christians who will survive the sorting that Jesus undertakes at the judgment.

Belonging to a church is one vital piece of the jigsaw that makes up being a Christian – but it isn't the only piece. We must carry on looking further.

Questions for reflection

1. Where have you seen a church working at its best? What made it so good?

Read John 15:1–10, where Jesus gives another picture of what the church is like. He is the vine, Christians are the branches, and we are to 'remain' in him (or 'abide in him' or 'stay connected to him' in different translations).

2. What happens to branches to make them more fruitful? What happens to branches that don't remain connected to the vine? Can you give examples?
3. How can we remain connected to Jesus (see verses 7, 9–10)? What might that mean for you?
4. Read verse 11. Why does Jesus tell us about the vine and branches? Would you say your relationship with God is characterized by joy?
5. Read Acts 2:42–47, and re-read the questions listed on pages 53–54. If you are a regular member at a church, how does your church measure up? If you're not a regular member at a church, do you know of any churches near you that could answer 'yes' to most of these questions? As part of your reflection on this chapter, why not go along this week?
6. Glance back through the chapter. Talk to God in your own words about something that's challenged or encouraged you.

Piece 3: Behaving

'I've been going to church for a couple of years now – the music's good; the teaching's inspiring; I've made some great friends. But the church has got it wrong in some pretty big ways. The Bible's very old, and times have moved on. Life is different now, and the church must keep up when it comes to things like sex. Otherwise it comes over as really judgmental and intolerant.' (Keiran, nineteen)

'I get fed up with lots of churchgoers. They say they're Christians, but the way they live doesn't match up. They're always in their holy huddles,

and never doing anything for the homeless, or campaigning about poverty in Africa. For me, being a Christian isn't about going to church and making a big fuss of it. It's about helping other people. That's what I do.' (Jean, fifty-four)

Recently, we took a video camera around our local area and asked people 'What is a Christian?' The most common responses were to do with how a person lives their life:

- 'A Christian practises the ideals of Christ – generally being a really good person.'
- 'A Christian treats others with respect and courtesy.'
- 'A Christian lives by most of the Ten Commandments.' (I didn't ask which of the ten were no longer relevant!)

But can Christianity really be reduced to just a set of values like respect, courtesy and tolerance? As we read Jesus' teaching, he doesn't just mention obligations such as feeding the hungry, visiting the sick and helping the homeless. In the Sermon on the Mount, he raised the bar even higher than it had been before:

- The existing law said, 'Do not murder', but Jesus added that 'anyone who is angry with his brother or sister will be subject to judgment'.[1]
- The existing law said, 'Do not commit adultery', but Jesus added that 'any man who looks at a woman lustfully has already committed adultery with her in his heart'.[2]
- The existing law said, 'Love your neighbour', but Jesus added, 'Love your enemies and pray for those who persecute you.'[3]

Common objections

Let's be honest: Jesus' clear teaching that genuine Christians are to seek to obey him in all areas of our lives is decidedly uncomfortable! It challenges our lifestyle, demanding change from us where we least want it. How often have I used (and heard others using) some of the following objections?

Objection 1: 'Jesus died to forgive me. Surely it won't matter if I carry on sinning?'

Some people think that it's as though God has opened a tab for us at the bar, and he's promised to pay the account in full at the end of the evening, no matter how many drinks we've had.

The poet Heinrich Heine said on his deathbed, 'Of course God will forgive me. It's his job.'[4] There is truth in that: God will not turn away anyone who turns to him, no matter what their background. If God can accept Saul, who'd been persecuting Christians and called himself 'the worst of sinners',[5] he can accept anyone! But we mustn't imagine that God's forgiveness is purely mechanical, like an unthinking, knee-jerk reaction.

Think about a time when someone has hurt you deeply. It's not easy to forgive them! Sometimes it takes people months or years to get to a point of being able to forgive, for the hurt is so personal and goes so deep. Forgiving someone costs us much emotional heartache. So it is with God. He made us, so he has a deep personal interest in each of us. When we ignore him and his will for our lives, it hurts him personally and deeply, so it's not easy for him to forgive us. It cost him the death of his Son to forgive us.

Think back to that person who's hurt you deeply. If you have managed to forgive them, how would you feel if they then went and did exactly the same thing again? If anything, it would be even harder to forgive them a second time around. And again, just because God has forgiven us, and has promised to go on forgiving us, it doesn't mean that it's easy for him to do so.

Dietrich Bonhoeffer, a German pastor executed by the Nazis, wrote that grace 'is costly because it cost God the life of his Son . . . and what has cost God much cannot be cheap for us'.[6] It's as though our salvation is free, but it costs us everything. Jesus certainly likened discovering the kingdom of God to discovering treasure hidden in a field – and selling everything one owns in order to purchase that field.[7] And he didn't just say, 'Follow me', but 'If anyone would come after me, he must deny himself and take up his cross and follow me.'[8]

So yes, there is a tab at the bar for us, and Jesus has paid it all. But it's as if he also says, 'If you love me, you'll keep the tab as low as possible!'

Right from the earliest days, Christians have asked, 'Shall we go on sinning so that grace may increase?' – to which the authoritative Christian answer has always been, 'By no means!'[9]

Objection 2: 'Didn't Jesus say he came to set me free from rules?'
People love the idea of a life without rules – at least, they do in theory. But if we stop to think about it, we know that a life without rules results in anarchy – and that's no fun for anyone. Imagine a school football game where a stand-in referee doesn't know the rules of the game: dangerous tackles are allowed, off-side goals are counted, clear penalties are waived. No-one would enjoy it! Clear rules, sensibly and fairly applied, are healthy.

The perception that Jesus came to set us free from rules is actually a subtle distortion of what he really said – that he'd come to set us free from *'slavery* to the law' (that is, he came to stop us trying to *earn* our way into heaven by obeying rules and regulations). Nowhere did Jesus say that he'd come to set us free from *obeying* God's law. On the contrary, he said, 'Do not think that I have come to abolish the Law or the Prophets; I have not come to abolish them but to fulfil them.'[10]

The apostle Paul made the nature of our freedom clear. Writing to Christians, he said: 'You were called to be free. But do not use your freedom to indulge the sinful nature; rather, serve one another in love.'[11] Christian freedom, then, isn't a freedom to live how *we* want (pleasing ourselves), but is freedom to live as *God* wants (pleasing God by serving him and others).

The reason he's given us the law is to help define what genuine love looks like. Keeping the law isn't meant to drag us down. 'The law is good if one uses it properly.'[12] It gives 'joy to the heart' and 'light to the eyes'.[13]

Real lives - Samantha

Samantha, thirty-one, is a marketing manager for a zoo.

A housemate dragged me to church a few times. One Sunday, I was singing away with everyone else and for no reason at all I suddenly started sobbing. It was like a syringe, pushing water out, and when I stopped I felt a rush of peace and contentment. It was like all the rubbish that I had been feeling had been pushed out. Although it happened several other times, I chose to ignore it and carry on with my life. For several years after this, I shied away from Christianity – I lost my mum at an early age, and I struggled with how God fitted into that – but I finally joined an Alpha course. The rest is history.

Since having a relationship with God, my life has been completely transformed. What surprised me the most about becoming a Christian is the total peace I feel. I used to watch people during services and see this happy look on their faces, wondering why I didn't feel that. I now know it's because I just didn't have faith in God. Although I had a belief and was open to the idea of God, I hadn't given my life up to him. It's not until you start letting go of your old self that you really start feeling God's hand on your life. When you do, it's amazing! I still struggle with this, but it's definitely getting easier.

I used to be a major party girl with my self-worth totally wrapped up in being accepted by others. Since becoming a Christian, God has slowly been working within me. I'm still very sociable, but I now see myself through God's eyes and I'm not half bad! What I originally thought were a lot of constrictive rules used to control people are actually God trying to help us. It's good for the soul when you manage it, but I'm not totally there yet!

Objection 3: 'Aren't the Bible's commands 2,000 years out of date?'

As society continues to move towards a less conservative understanding of what constitutes 'acceptable behaviour', this objection is getting more and more common. But although the Ten Commandments were given by God in a certain time and place, 3,500 years ago, they are universally applicable. Jesus himself endorsed them 1,500 years after they were initially given (i.e. in a very different age and culture), and the first church leaders upheld them for use amongst the Jewish, Roman and Greek cultures of the day.

We shouldn't think of the Ten Commandments as a *human* invention, but we should recognize them as given by our Maker, who alone knows best how we function as humans. Nor should we think of them as *time-bound*, but should recognize them as given by the Eternal One, whose wisdom will always be true and good for us, no matter what culture we inhabit or what language we speak. For example, as our culture moves towards an increasing 24/7 work pattern, it's been accompanied by an increase in stress and a decrease in happiness. ('Tell me about it,' I can hear some of you say!) But of course God prescribed regular time off and holidays for us because he knows that we need time out to refocus and recharge.

Objection 4: 'I've messed up big time already. There's no point trying to start being holy now.'

Sometimes people confide in me some of the mistakes they've made in the past. My heart always goes out to them, for they're often weighed down by a huge burden of guilt – and regret. For those who suffer from low self-esteem or depression, it seems to be only a downward spiral.

Of course, we can't quickly forget mistakes we've made, and we sometimes have to live with the consequences for years. But God can, and does, forgive our sin, wipe away our guilt and give us hope of a different future. He specifically called people who'd messed up to follow him. For example, he told a woman who was having an adulterous affair, 'Leave your life of sin.'[14] When a swindler decided to follow Jesus, he announced, 'If I have cheated anybody out of anything, I will pay back four times the amount.'[15] None of us is perfect when we come to Jesus. But God promises his people that, 'Though your sins are like scarlet, they shall be as white as snow; though they are red as crimson, they shall be like wool.'[16]

So just because we've made mistakes is no reason not to renew our commitment to living God's way. In fact, sometimes it's all the more reason to make that commitment – for we know all too well the damage done to ourselves and to others by not living as God asks us.

Objection 5: 'But I don't want to change!'

This is perhaps the most honest objection; the others may really be excuses. To say 'I don't want to change' reveals our heart – we are too comfortable as we are to want to live differently.

The person who says this recognizes that genuine Christian faith always impinges on our private lives and makes us uncomfortable. Jesus encouraged would-be followers to consider carefully the cost of following him before embarking on the journey. 'Suppose one of you wants to build a tower,' Jesus said. 'Won't you first sit down and estimate the cost to see if you have enough money to complete it? For if you lay the foundation and are not able to finish it, everyone who sees it will ridicule you, saying, "This person began to build and wasn't able to finish."' We must work out if we're willing to sacrifice our comforts and pleasures to follow Jesus. As he concluded, 'Those of you who do not give up everything you have cannot be my disciples.'[17]

When I struggle in this area, I need to remind myself that changing my behaviour and character to become more like Jesus won't cramp my life! I need to remember that God is my loving Father, who wants only the best for me. To remember that living as my Maker intended is the way to find true blessing. To remember that God's law is good, giving joy to the heart. To remember that the 'pleasures of sin' last but 'a short time',[18] whilst enjoying God is my *eternal* privilege. To remember Jesus' warning and promise: 'For whoever wants to save their life will lose it, but whoever loses their life for me and for the gospel will save it.'[19] To remember that Jesus came that I 'may have life and have it to the full'.[20]

When we remember all those things, we'll see that the sensible thing to do is to accept Jesus' teaching, and submit all parts of our lives to his lordship as a sign of our love for him.

What motivates Christians to behave like Jesus?

Here are four positive reasons Jesus gives as to why we should follow his teaching about how we live our lives.

Motivation 1: We comply with Jesus' commands as a mark of our love for him

Throughout the Bible, God has called his people to love him. When Jesus said the most important commandment is to love him, he wasn't referring to a gooey, emotional sort of love (although that is part of it). True love is always practical. If my wife asks me to stop a bad habit (putting my feet on the table/ picking my nose/belching, etc. – not that I'd ever do those things, of course!), and I truly love her, I will do as she asks. So it is with Jesus. 'If you love me,' said Jesus to his followers, 'you will obey what I command.'[21] So Christians adopt Jesus' standards of behaviour as a sign of our love for him. To disobey is a sign that we don't love him.

Of course, we only love him 'because he first loved us'.[22] It's important to understand in this talk of obedience to Jesus that he came to bring us true *life*. God 'sent his one and only Son into the world that we might *live* through him'.[23] So many people assume that following God's commandments will be terribly restrictive, and sap all the fun out of life. In fact, quite the opposite is true.

Living as God designed us to live is actually the way to get the most out of life. God isn't a hard taskmaster, who wants to make our life a misery. He's a loving Father, who lays down boundaries to protect us and help us enjoy life. Our two-year-old likes playing with electric plug sockets, but we don't let him. That's not because we want to take away his enjoyment of life, but precisely because we lovingly want to protect and preserve his life!

Jason Robinson, the former England rugby star, expressed this well. Prior to becoming a Christian, he had a typically rich party lifestyle, fuelled by lots of alcohol. After becoming a Christian, he wrote: 'People often think that because of my devotion to Christianity, my life must be restricted, but I feel freer now than I have ever done.'[24]

There is only one way Jesus has asked us to express our love for him. It's not by singing songs to him! 'This is love for God: to obey his commands. And his commands are not burdensome.'[25] If we've understood this, to go on sinning deliberately is a sign of our lack of love for God.

Real lives – Amy

Amy, thirty-one, is an environmental contamination geologist and volunteer worker with homeless people.

I was raised to go to Sunday school, but keeping religion very firmly 'in its box'. By my teens I had branded Christianity as irrelevant and many Christians as hypocrites, and decided that God did not exist.

As a student, a growing sense of the wonder of creation led me to determine that I did believe in God after all. I became friends with several dedicated Christians – I found their commitment, gentleness, kindness and clear humanity intriguing.

After my divorce, and with the chance to start life anew, I went on an Alpha course. I remember being asked to re-imagine my world with God at the centre – rather than me at the centre. It made me realize that I didn't think I needed anyone or anything to intercede for me – but maybe God saw it differently. A few months later, I became a Christian – somewhat reluctantly, as it required a great deal of humility!

I was really surprised when I discovered that 'Christian behaviour' is a response to Christ, rather than a require-ment of Christ. I used to think you had to do God's will to 'earn' his love. I've spent the last few years 'unlearning' that wrong thinking. Now I try to keep God's command-ments and love others – out of thanksgiving – because I know God loves me and has forgiven me. It's incredibly freeing to know that my faith in Christ is all that is required – everything else naturally flows from that.

The church I attend now feels positive, vibrant, welcom-ing, inclusive. It's a Christian family, where I belong, where I am loved for who I am, warts and all. It's incredibly freeing and not like anything else I have experienced.

Motivation 2: We behave like Jesus because we represent him to others

Imagine you're chosen to represent your country at the Olympics in your favourite sport. What an honour! But suppose, in your desire to perform well, you take illegal performance-enhancing drugs, and get found out. You don't just bring shame on yourself, but on your country.

Probably many times I've done things that have made people think, 'He's not a very good Christian, is he?' In short, I've been a hypocrite. It turns out that one of the loudest critics of religious hypocrisy is Jesus himself. He couldn't stand it! Speaking to religious leaders, he lambasted their double standards: 'On the outside you appear to people as righteous but on the inside you are full of hypocrisy and wickedness . . . greed and self-indulgence.'[26]

But I fear that on occasion when I've hurt others, people have even thought, 'If that's what you're like, I don't want anything to do with your God, thank you very much.' Can you see how failing to live as Jesus asks doesn't just bring shame on ourselves, but brings God into disrepute as well? It makes me so sad to think that people might think less of God because of things I've said and done.

But it works the other way round as well: Jesus said, 'By this all people will know you are my disciples: if you love one another.'[27] In other words, the more we live a life of love as Jesus did, the more people will recognize us as belonging to Jesus – and give credit to him.

In fact, throughout the Bible, God has called his people to be like him in their character and actions. For example, we're to be truthful, faithful, loving and committed to justice, because God himself is those things. In short, God calls his people to 'Be holy, because I am holy.'[28] Jesus himself reiterated this call: 'Be perfect, therefore, as your heavenly Father is perfect.'[29] Jesus wants us to become more like him, so to carry on sinning is to reject God's desire for our lives.

Motivation 3: When we act as Jesus did – serving others – we serve Jesus himself

A few years ago, my dad had a heart attack on the streets of

London. Fortunately, someone came to his aid and he was in hospital within minutes. If I ever met that person, I'd want to thank them profusely, because in helping my dad, they've served me and our whole family.

When Christians serve others (feeding the homeless, campaigning about poverty, taking medical supplies where they're needed, etc.), our motivation isn't just that we know Jesus is concerned about issues of justice and mercy. He offers us a deeper motivation, too: as we have compassion on others, it's as though we're serving Jesus himself, just as the person who helped my dad served me.

Jesus told one of his most famous parables to make this very point.[30] He was picturing the end of time when he will pronounce his judgment on each one of us – to let us know on what grounds he will make that judgment. To some he will say, 'Come . . . take your inheritance, the kingdom prepared for you . . . For I was hungry and you gave me something to eat, I was thirsty and you gave me something to drink, I was a stranger and you invited me in, I needed clothes and you clothed me, I was sick and you looked after me, I was in prison and you came to visit me.' But as he explains, the actions he's remembering are actually those they 'did for one of the least of these brothers and sisters of mine'. By contrast, Jesus will say to everyone else, 'Depart from me . . . into the eternal fire', because they didn't have compassion on those in need.

Jesus is reminding us again that he alone determines our eternal destiny. Whether *we* think of ourselves as Christians is irrelevant; what's important is whether *Jesus* does. One of his criteria is whether we show practical compassion to those in need. We should do – because as we do, we serve Jesus himself. What higher motivation could there be?!

Motivation 4: We obey what Jesus says because he is our Lord

To say 'Jesus is Lord' is to say 'Jesus is my boss'. It's not just to recognize that Jesus, as God, is the rightful ruler over all creation; it's also to recognize that he's the rightful ruler of *my* life, and to submit myself to him. And if Jesus is my boss, I'm not really in a position to negotiate with him! Jesus himself said to his followers, 'You call me "Teacher" and "Lord", and rightly so, for that is what I am.'[31] So we are to listen to him as our Teacher, and then obey him as our Lord.

Slowly but surely, Jesus will want to bring every area of our lives under his lordship. He will want to bring change to our lips and the language that we use; to our eyes and the things that we look at; to our ears and the people and ideas we listen to. He will want to bring change to our hearts, shaping what we love; to our minds, shaping how we think; to our hands, shaping how we act. He will want to take up residence in our workplaces, influencing our attitudes to work; in our bedrooms, influencing our closest relationships; in our leisure, influencing how we use our money.

Real lives - Trevor

Trevor, thirty-three, is a safety engineering consultant, comic book fan and DIY fanatic.

For me, becoming a Christian was a very slow, progressive experience, which built up over a number of years. As a teenager I never really liked church. When I moved to England, I joined a church where I went on an Alpha course. Soon after that I realized that I would never have all the answers, but I knew enough to trust in God and make that step of faith. I became a Christian later that year at the age of twenty-four.

I used to struggle a lot with anger. Like so many men I hid my anger behind a plastic smile, but I soon realized that the anger was creating problems in my life. It was destructive – a barrier between me and God. Since becoming a Christian and studying God's Word, I have learned that my anger was in effect revealing aspects of my life that I needed to work on, correct and allow to be transformed by God's grace. By slowly realigning my life with the gospel I have started to take responsibility for my anger – dealing with it constructively instead of allowing it to rob me of my happiness.

At the conclusion to the Sermon on the Mount, Jesus issued a stark warning to those who admired his words, and even claimed faith in him, but who disobeyed: 'Not everyone who says to me, "Lord, Lord," will enter the kingdom of heaven, but only *the one who does the will of my Father* who is in heaven.' He warned that not even active Christian ministry makes up for such disobedience: 'Many will say to me on that day, "Lord, Lord, did we not prophesy in your name, and in your name drive out demons and perform many miracles?" Then I will tell them plainly, "I never knew you. Away from me, you evildoers!"'[32]

The message is clear: if we claim to be Christians, calling Jesus 'Lord', we must obey him. If we persistently carry on sinning, it reveals that there are areas of our lives where Jesus isn't yet Lord.

Wrong motivation: We don't obey Jesus to earn his approval
We must conclude this section by emphasizing that Christian obedience *isn't* a way of gaining Jesus' approval – although many people mistakenly think it is. They are under the notion that their 'good works' can earn their place in heaven. But nothing could be further from the truth. Do you remember the picture of the ladder we looked at in piece 1? God is so holy (at the top of the ladder) and we are so sinful (near the bottom) that we will never come close to God's heavenly standards. However much harder we try to lead a good life, we will only ever be a few rungs further up the ladder – and we'll never succeed in being good enough to get to the top. Rather, we are saved by God's grace – his loving, undeserved gift.

When one man, who'd previously been trying hard to earn God's approval, realized this, and let its truth sink into his heart, he said, 'I felt a release and a liberation unlike anything I had ever felt before. Finally, my feet weren't building blisters on the treadmill of good works. I was lifted off the tightrope of the fear of death and punishment, and instead cast upon the sure ground and security of an outrageous love that came with no strings attached.'[33]

Ultimately, Christianity isn't about what *we* do for *Christ*, but about what *he* has done for *us*. Trusting in his death is what wins our salvation. But *having been saved*, we now seek to please him as a sign of our new love for him, in order to become more like him, and as a sign of our new submission to him as Lord.

How can I change?

Let's suppose that you've been convinced that Jesus' teaching about how we live our lives is far more challenging than you previously realized, yet also far more liberating. You'd like to start living more in line with God's commandments as a sign of your love for him. Maybe God's put his finger on a particular area of your life that needs to change if you're to live as a genuine Christian: a wrong relationship that needs to be reformed; an addiction (e.g. alcohol, pornography or drugs) that needs to end; a character trait (e.g. quick temper, lack of compassion) that needs to be refined. How exactly can we achieve such change?

1. *Be reassured that change is possible!* Countless Christians through the ages have seen God change their lives in remarkable ways. No-one is beyond God's power. Some change happens quickly; most change takes months and years. He's got a long way to go with me!

2. *Pray regularly.* Jesus knew that we would face many temptations, so he taught us to pray, 'Lead us not into temptation.'[34] I find that a really helpful prayer. As we ask God for his help, we open ourselves to being transformed by him.

3. *Co-operate with God's Spirit.* As we let God work in us, the result is 'love, joy, peace, patience, kindness, goodness, faithfulness, gentleness and self-control'.[35] Imagine you're faced with a steep icy slope, and you're trying to get to the top. It's impossible by yourself! Yet that's what resisting temptation can feel like – an impossible task. One minute we make progress; the next, we slide back down. What the Holy Spirit does is fit us with crampons – the spiked grips that mountaineers use on their shoes to help them climb on ice. It's the Holy Spirit who gives us the grip to resist the downward pull of temptation. But of course, a mountaineer's crampons

by themselves are useless. They have to be fitted to the boots, and the climber has to move his or her legs before any upward progress is made. So it is with us: we must rely on the Holy Spirit (letting him transform us), but also work hard ourselves, before we become more like Christ.

4. *Don't get discouraged by failures.* We mustn't let ourselves become paralysed with guilt at our failures. Jesus taught us to pray frequently, 'Forgive us our debts',[36] knowing that we would often sin. His promise of forgiveness will never wear out: 'If we confess our sins, [God] is faithful and just and will forgive us our sins.'[37]

Is 'behaving' enough?

If a terrible accident happened, and you were to die tonight, and Jesus were to say to you, 'Why should I let you into my heaven?', what would you say?

It's a sobering thought, but a question we will all face one day. There will be no-one else to answer on our behalf. It'll just be Jesus looking us in the eye, asking why he should let us in. What would you say?

Most people's tendency is to reach into their past and highlight the goodness of their lives: 'I didn't hurt other people'; 'I didn't cheat in my exams'; 'I cared for my ageing parents with no reward'; 'I gave money to charity'; 'I drove an eco-friendly car'; 'I tried my best.'

Some people say they would draw Jesus' attention to their religious observance: 'I was baptized and confirmed'; 'I prayed to you faithfully'; 'I took communion regularly.'

But Jesus would look at someone giving those sorts of answers with a sad expression on his face. At the end of their list of good works, he would shake his head, and say, 'You can't come in.'

'Why not?!' you might say, incredulously.

Well, do you remember how I said earlier that we *don't* behave in order to impress Jesus, or in order to gain his favour? But that's exactly what those answers are trying to do! Try as we might, we'll never be able to climb high enough to get to heaven by our own good works. We might boast that we never hurt anyone, but then Jesus would gently remind us of that time we deliberately annoyed our neighbour. We might boast about looking after ageing parents, but then Jesus would point out that our attitude towards them was not always one of love but of resentment. The standard for entry into heaven is perfection, and none of us is perfect.

Rather, Jesus has climbed down the rope ladder from heaven to us. In his death, he paid the penalty for our sins. And he offers us a piggy-back ride up the ladder into heaven. We can enter only by trusting him.

So when Jesus asks us 'Why should I let you enter my heaven?', the genuine Christian will answer, 'I'm not worthy to enter your heaven, Jesus. But I trust that you died for me, so that I may come in.' As Martin Luther used to say, 'Heaven isn't a reward, but a gift.'

Yes, Christians seek to behave as Jesus tells us. But we do so as a *response* of love to him, because he first loved us. We do so as a sign of submission to him as Lord, because he has first been our Saviour. A Christian who *doesn't* seek to behave as Jesus wants them to live is missing a vital piece of the jigsaw. But a person who *only* has this piece of the jigsaw is sadly mistaken when they think that their good behaviour will get them to heaven. As Jesus said, 'Love your neighbour as yourself' is only the *second* most important command.[38]

Questions for reflection

1. Would you say that you lead a good life? If so, what is your motivation for doing so? How does that compare to the motivations given on pages 67–74?

   Read Luke 10:25–37, the popular parable of the Good Samaritan. The man is keen to 'inherit eternal life' – i.e. to be counted as a Christian.

2. Jesus tells this parable to encourage the man to love anyone in need. What might this mean in your context?
3. What else did Jesus say the man needed to do? (See also John 14:15.) Would you say that you love God/Jesus? If so, how?

   Read Luke 18:9–14, a parable Jesus told.

4. What evidence is there that the Pharisee behaved impeccably? So why did Jesus condemn him?
5. By contrast, what do we know about the tax collector's behaviour? So why did Jesus applaud him? What do you think Jesus' verdict on you would be?
6. Glance back through the chapter. Talk to God in your own words about something that's challenged or encouraged you.

Piece 4: Baptism

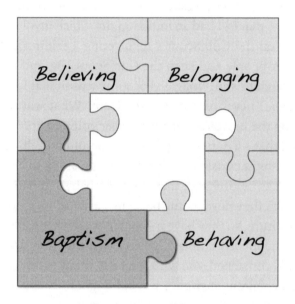

'I was christened when I was a baby, so I know I'm a Christian. I think it's left me with a sense of right and wrong, which I try to live by. I never got confirmed, and don't really see the need to. My faith is between me and God. It's when people start talking about their faith too loudly that arguments or even wars start. I think it's best when religion is kept private.' (Terry, seventy-four)

'I've been going along to church for a few years now. At first, I was a bit nervous. Now, I look forward to seeing my friends there. I *understand much more now about what goes on, and it's become more meaningful to me. Sometimes they christen babies, who usually scream the church down! I realized recently that I'd never been christened – but I'm not sure if adults are allowed.' (Gayle, thirty-three)*

When I was young, I went along to the Cubs – a junior member of the famous Scout Association. After a few months, I was 'invested' – that is, I had an initiation rite which involved laying my hand on the Cub Scout flag, uttering a solemn pledge to help other people and keep the Cub Scout law, and receiving my neckerchief and 'woggle'. For some reason that I now can't remember, I never returned to the Cubs! What was the point of joining the movement if I was never going to go?

Sadly, that's a pattern repeated all too often in this country when a baby is christened. The parents go along to church for a few weeks beforehand, then have the baby's initiation rite – after which they never come back! Just as I had misunderstood my investiture, so they have misunderstood what a christening implies and involves. In fact, when asked why they are getting their child christened, and what it means, many parents struggle to give a coherent answer. 'I wanted to get my baby done' is a common phrase that covers up much confusion!

What is baptism?

The Bible uses the word 'baptism' rather than 'christening'. 'To baptize' literally means 'to dip or plunge'. Every week around the world, thousands of adults come to faith in Christ and are baptized – some are plunged fully and briefly into a river, the sea or a pool in a church building; others (normally babies) have water sprinkled over them. To people who haven't a clue what's going on, it must look very strange! Why would someone voluntarily get dunked in the cold sea? Or why would a parent let a stranger sprinkle water over their baby with the resulting tears?

Think for a moment of the Queen. When did she become Queen? Was it when her father, the King, died? Or was it when she was crowned a few months later? The answer is that she became Queen the moment her father died. That's when the privileges, powers and responsibilities of monarchy became hers. Her coronation was simply the public ceremony that acknowledged the Queen's new status.

A baptism is similar. The privileges, powers and responsibilities of being children of God are ours as soon as we are adopted by God into his family. The baptism is simply the public ceremony that acknowledges a Christian's new status, stemming from the inner change of heart involved in becoming a Christian.

As it does when talking about 'church', the Bible uses several images to build up our overall picture of what baptism means.

1. Baptism is a sign of washing

People and things get dirty. Having just bathed my children and dealt with several loads of washing, I'm all too aware of that! We wash to get clean, and the Bible pictures baptism as a sign of being washed clean from sin. Whether the washing is a sprinkling from above (like a shower) or a full immersion in water (like going under in a bath) doesn't matter. Both get us clean. As soon as Saul (later known as the apostle Paul) became a Christian, he was told to 'be baptised and wash your sins away, calling on [Jesus'] name'.[1]

Sin is likened to dirt; the inner change of becoming a Christian has the effect of washing our sins away, so that we are considered clean and pure. God describes such forgiveness like this: 'Though your sins are like scarlet, they shall be as white as snow;

though they are red as crimson, they shall be like wool.'[2] It sounds like an advert for a wonderful new washing powder! – one that gets us spiritually clean, washing away our sin and guilt.

However, whereas we wash ourselves in the shower, no-one baptizes themselves. It is *God* who forgives us and washes us – by Jesus' death. Jesus himself described his death as a baptism he had to go through.[3] It was the supreme baptism when Jesus dealt with our sin once for all, so that we may be forgiven.

This picture of baptism highlights the Christian's need for God's forgiveness. For someone to be baptized, then, they should

1. recognize that they are sinful;
2. desire to be forgiven;
3. know that such forgiveness can come only because of Jesus' sacrificial death, not through any effort of their own;
4. trust personally in Jesus' death for their own forgiveness.

Real lives – Victoria

Victoria, twenty-two, is a PhD student by day and a clubber by night.

Last year, a friend took me along to a Christmas service at his church, which I really enjoyed, and which started me thinking about Christianity. I had never considered myself an atheist; I had always liked to believe that there was something more to life. Soon after, another friend became a Christian – I decided to take a proper look at why she had. Around this time, I went to a few more services at church. I found I enjoyed them, and that the sermons made sense. I went on a Christianity Explored course, which just helped me affirm that I wanted to live my life for Christ. I was surprised to find that you don't have to be perfect! One of the most powerful messages from the course was about God's grace: that he will forgive us no matter what we do.

One of the best moments since then was getting baptized. It was the most wonderful experience to be able to declare my faith publicly to everyone, including my parents and my friends. The symbolism of dying to sin and being reborn into a life where you have a relationship with Jesus is something that can only give you hope.

It's not always been easy. I came up against opposition from my family and friends, who clearly thought I had taken leave of my senses. Slowly, they realized that fundamentally I am the same person, although the focus of my life has changed. To begin with, I felt a lot of guilt about the way I had been living, and as I looked at my life, I kept seeing more and more that was wrong with how I had been living my life. I know now that God forgives me for that simply because I have asked him to, and now I try to live my life in a way that pleases him.

2. Baptism is a sign of Jesus' death – and ours!

I once nearly knocked someone out doing a full immersion baptism. We'd hired in a special pool (a bit like a birthing pool) to our church building, but the pool was quite small and the chap was quite tall. As I leaned him backwards into the water, his head hit the side of the pool. He was, in fact, absolutely fine – but I remember the mother of the lad I was about to baptize next looking decidedly nervous as he climbed into the pool!

Of course, if that chap had been injured, it would have been terrible. But the next picture the Bible uses for baptism is far more extreme. *Death* is the last thing most people expect a baptism to signify – especially if it's a newborn baby being baptized! But this graphic image is what is implied as a believer is plunged fully into water – it is a sign of death. Some churches even have baptism pools in the shape of a coffin!

Jesus himself had said that his followers must 'deny themselves and take up their cross daily'[4] – a vivid picture of personal death. Following on from this, the apostle Paul asked, 'Do you not know that all of us who were baptised into Christ Jesus were baptised into his death?'[5] How do we deny ourselves, and in what way do we die? Michael Green writes:

> Baptism means death to the person I once was, self-centred, unforgiven, alienated from the life of God. Goodbye to all that . . . And death *means* death. At times it will be devastating: death to your hopes, dreams and ambitions. It may mean death to a work you have built up and seen flourish. It will mean death, all along the line, to self-will.[6]

In British culture, baptism doesn't tend to be perceived as signalling such a radical change of life; it's seen merely as a naming ceremony or entry rite. But the sacrifices involved in getting baptized can be huge. I've had the privilege of baptizing academics from mainland China, who know that by merely being baptized, they risk academic suicide, for promotions tend to go to Communist Party members rather than Christian believers. Similarly, I've been privileged to baptize an Iranian asylum seeker who converted from Islam to Christianity. He knew when he was baptized that if he was ever deported back to Iran, his new faith could put his very life at risk. Indeed, when a Muslim or Jew converts to following Jesus, it's not uncommon for their family to hold a funeral for them! It is a painful experience to know that your family is counting you as dead, but it shows that they've understood what you've done: you've decisively left your old lifestyle and religion.

This picture of baptism highlights the radical change of priorities involved in becoming a Christian. When someone is baptized, they are pledging total loyalty to Jesus, who bids us come and die. Following him will not be easy. At times it will involve great personal sacrifice.

3. Baptism is a sign of Jesus' resurrection – and ours

Just as Jesus didn't remain dead in the grave, nor does the person being immersed in water remain under water! Paul said, 'We were therefore buried with him through baptism into death in order that, just as Christ was raised from the dead . . . we too may live a new life. If we have been united with him in a death like his, we will certainly also be united with him in a resurrection like his.'[7] In other words, having died to our old way of life, Christians rise to a new life shared with Jesus and governed by him, a life that will never end.

The great encouragement is that the same power that raised Jesus from death now works in the Christian to help them conquer sin and live a life pleasing to God. Professor J. I. Packer puts it like this: 'Receiving the sign in faith assures the persons baptised that God's gift of new life in Christ is freely given to them. At the same time, it commits them to live henceforth in a new way as committed disciples of Jesus.'[8]

This picture of baptism highlights God's power at work in a Christian's life. In baptism, believers commit themselves to living a new, Jesus-shaped life, in the full expectation that, in due course, Jesus will raise them from the dead to share his eternal glory.

I love baptizing adults, for there's a real sense of celebration in a baptism service. It's great to hear some of those being baptized share something of their story of faith in Christ; it's lovely to see family and friends come along to support them (even if some are a bit dubious about their friend's faith!); for the church family, it's a wonderful opportunity to celebrate the promises of forgiveness and new life that God gives to each believer. There's normally lots of applause and a great time of praise to God.

4. Baptism links us to Christ in membership

If you're a member of a local football team, you pay your subs, and in return you get to train together, wear the team's kit, play for the team (if you're good enough!), and have your say at the annual meeting as to how the team should be run. Baptism is also a sign of membership, but it is a much *deeper* level of membership. In a football team, the members are, at the end of the day, separate human beings, who are merely happy to be associated with each other by way of their common passion. Baptism points to the person becoming part of Christ Jesus himself: they are 'baptised *into* Christ'.[9] Or, as Jesus put it, we are baptized 'in the name of the Father and of the Son and of the Holy Spirit'.[10]

In our culture, a person's name carries little weight – it's just what they're called. So if I (heaven forbid!) baptized someone 'into Dan', it wouldn't make much sense. In Jesus' day, someone's name conveyed much more meaning – it referred to their whole character. So to baptize someone 'into Christ' would have been understood as this person coming under Jesus' authority and adopting his character, by being associated with his name.

Being baptized, then, indicates that someone hasn't just died *with* Christ and been raised *with* Christ, but that they somehow now live *in* Christ, and Christ *in* them. If you like, the baptism highlights the permanent change of status that takes place when a person becomes a Christian – they are adopted into God's family – and can never be un-adopted!

A *watershed moment*

Taking all this together, baptism is clearly an *initiation* rite: it marks the end of an old way of life, and the beginning of a new life – a life lived under Jesus' authority, in Jesus' power. It quite literally marks a watershed moment in someone's life. It should be a sign of no return to the former life. As such, baptism is probably better understood in cultures dominated by other religions.

Getting from symbol to reality

Think back to the Queen and her coronation. When the crown was put on her head, it symbolized the fact that she really was Queen, and had been since her father died. The crown was merely the visible symbol of the change that had already happened. But what would have happened if Prince Philip had snatched the crown and put it on his head? That wouldn't have made him king – for he wasn't the heir to the throne. The symbol and the reality have to match up for the symbol to be effective.

So it is with baptism. The water is the visible symbol of the inner change of heart that happens when someone becomes a Christian. But if the inner reality is absent, the symbol and the reality don't match up – so the water means about as much as putting the crown on Prince Philip's head.

The Bible records one such occasion where the symbol of baptism didn't match the reality of a changed heart. A man called Simon Magus, who said he believed in Christ, and who was baptized, showed he wasn't yet a genuine Christian by trying to buy God's Holy Spirit![11]

Sadly, there are many today, probably thousands or even millions, who have been baptized, but who aren't genuine Christians. A bishop, Tom Wright, notes, 'Not everyone who has been through water-baptism has actually known and experienced for themselves the saving love of God in Christ sweeping through and transforming their lives.'[12] The visible symbol of baptism doesn't match up to a changed heart. So how should symbol and reality be linked?

A look at the world's very first Christian baptism service gives us the answer. It was the 'Day of Pentecost', and Jewish believers were gathered from many nations. The apostle Peter preached to the crowd about Jesus' death and resurrection, and about people's own sinfulness before God. At the end of the sermon, we're told that 'When the people heard this, they were cut to the heart and said to Peter and the other apostles, "Brothers, what shall we do?" Peter replied, "Repent and be baptised, every one of you, in the name of Jesus Christ for the forgiveness of your sins. And you will receive the gift of the Holy Spirit."' The result was that 'Those who accepted his message were baptised, and about three thousand were added to their number that day.'[13] It was a pretty big baptism service!

Here's what was going on: the invisible *inner* change in the people was that they were 'cut to the heart' about their sin, and so 'repented'. That is, they turned away from their sin and turned to Christ for forgiveness. The *outward* symbol of that repentance was being baptized in Jesus' name. Two things *linked* the inner change and outward symbol: *faith* in Christ and the gift of the *Holy Spirit*.

This pattern is repeated in all the Bible's descriptions of people becoming genuine Christians. 'The norm of Christian experience is a cluster of four things: repentance, faith in Jesus, water baptism and the gift of the Spirit. Though the perceived order may vary a little, the four belong together and are universal in Christian initiation.'[14]

So when an *adult* is baptized, they give voice to their inner heart-change, in words of repentance and faith. When a *baby* is baptized (christened), their parents express repentance and faith on the baby's behalf. Not all Christians agree that it is right to baptize babies in this way, but every Christian desires that these babies come to repentance and faith when they become adults[15] and receive the gift of the Spirit[16] – because the outward sign of baptism is meaningless without the inner heart of repentance and faith in Christ and the wonderful gift of the Spirit.

Suppose you're presented with a cheque for a million pounds as a gift. It is extremely valuable! You're probably already thinking what you would do with the money. Yet whilst the cheque remains in your pocket, it is worthless. It is, after all, just a piece of paper. What makes it valuable is the promise it represents: 'I promise to pay the bearer on demand £1,000,000.' You would be daft not to claim the promise by cashing the cheque!

So it is with baptism: it is an extremely valuable gift! We do nothing to deserve it; it is purely out of God's generosity that he gives it to us. It represents enormous promises from God – his promise to forgive us our sins, to crucify our sinful nature with Christ, to raise us with Christ to resurrection life, to take us 'into him' for all eternity, never to be rejected. Yet at the end of the day, baptism is just some water – worthless. What makes the baptism real, what makes the promises come true, is when we, by faith in Christ, cash the cheque.

If you've been baptized, or christened as a baby, have you cashed the cheque? You'd be foolish not to! But you must take hold of God's promises, given to you visibly in baptism, by faith.

As you do so, God will pour out his Spirit on you (a theme we'll explore more in the next chapter).

Real lives - Lindsey

Lindsey, forty, is a full-time mum.

As a child, my only knowledge of Jesus was through that film with Robert Powell, and one trip to Sunday school, which I didn't like at all!

During a long period of depression, I read the Bible. I felt God's presence during that time, but wasn't really willing to deal with what that might mean, so I was 'scared off'.

Last year, I was invited on a Christianity Explored course. I enjoyed it, but wasn't convinced that Christianity was for me, until we did the session on God's grace. That really affected me, and I started praying every night. After three weeks or so, I started to feel God's presence again, and this time I couldn't deny it, or what it meant. I had to admit to myself that I was becoming a Christian – no-one was more surprised by this than me! I started to attend church and read the Bible. I told my family and friends, who've been very supportive.

I've been amazed by how 'right' it all feels, and I honestly wish I'd found God sooner in my life. Things have changed a lot since I've become a Christian – I'm much more sociable now and have many more friends. I feel much happier in myself, and I don't worry like I used to. I renewed my baptism vows in March and that felt really right and rather wonderful! I am still blown away when I think about what Jesus did for me.

I used to think that belief in God was a delusion, or was something I'd never be capable of – I didn't see how people could be so certain of something that felt so unreal to me. Now I know God is with me, and the most astonishing thing is that all I had to do was take a couple of small steps towards him, and he welcomed me as though he'd always been waiting for me.

Why should Christians be baptized?

But maybe you've never been baptized. That might be because you're not ready to 'sign up' for all that baptism entails – especially the stuff about dying to self! Fair enough. But for some people, who have a genuine faith in Christ and are living for him day by day, it is simply because they have never got round to it. Or maybe they think that it isn't necessary – if it's just a bit of water, why make a fuss over it?

Let me give you some quick reasons why genuine Christians should be baptized:

- *As a mark of obedience to Jesus.* His final instruction to his disciples was 'Go and make disciples of all nations, baptising them in the name of the Father and of the Son and of the Holy Spirit . . . '[17] Jesus clearly wanted those who become his followers to be baptized. As it happens, my mother-in-law grew up as a member of the Salvation Army – a denomination that doesn't perform baptisms. She made a personal public commitment to Christ as a teenager (which she understood as equivalent to baptism,

although it didn't involve water), and has never wavered
from her faith in God and commitment to him and his
church. But over the last few years, after watching other
Christians get baptized, and hearing parts of the Bible
that talk about baptism, she felt a calling by God to be
baptized with water herself.

- *As a mark of your trust in God.* Baptism isn't something that
we do; it is something that is done *to us*. It is, therefore, a
very powerful sign that being a Christian isn't about what
we do, but about what God has done *for us*. In highlighting
God's gracious gift to us, it allows no room for pride in
our own goodness.

- *As a mark that you and others can remember.* Members
of the armed forces often go abroad on tours of duty
for months at a time. I'm sure that the spouse left at
home during that long spell might not *feel* married –
but a quick glance at their wedding ring reminds
them that they *are*. Similarly, being able to look back
to your baptism will reassure you that God has claimed
you for his own. That's useful on days when you
doubt that you're a Christian. Baptism also makes
it very clear to those who know you that being a
Christian isn't just a phase you're going through, or a
hobby, but is your wholehearted life-long commitment
to Christ.

Baptism is an important piece of the jigsaw that makes up a
genuine Christian. There are a few instances where genuine
Christians haven't been baptized.[18] For example, a criminal
executed on the cross next to Jesus said, 'Remember me when
you come into your kingdom.' In response, Jesus reassured
him, 'Today you will be with me in paradise'[19] – yet presumably

this man was never baptized! Other instances might include deathbed conversions – but these should be seen as exceptions that prove the rule. If someone is a genuine Christian, there would have to be a very good reason for them not to get baptized!

Someone amusingly described a baptism service as:

- a *gospel* service in which we receive God's forgiveness and salvation;
- a *marriage* service in which we become wedded to Christ as covenant partners;
- a *burial* service that signals death to our old self, and calls us to live henceforth by the Spirit;
- an *Easter* festival proclaiming Jesus' resurrection and ours;
- a *birthday* celebration of our new birth in Christ;
- an *admission* ceremony as we enter into the family of God;
- a *commissioning* service sending us out to a life wholly given to Christ in service.[20]

If you're a Christian, and that doesn't whet your appetite for getting baptized, nothing will!

Is baptism enough?

We've already seen that baptism, by itself, doesn't make someone a genuine Christian. The outward sign, by itself, is empty without an inner heart of repentance. Typically, if someone is baptized as an adult, the inner conviction comes first, then the outward sign. If someone has been baptized as a baby, the outward sign comes first and then needs to be joined by the inner conviction.

The order doesn't especially matter; what's important is that both parts are present!

But still more is needed as well. Jesus himself, when he spoke about baptism, made it clear that it's only part of genuine Christian discipleship. His final words were:

> All authority in heaven and on earth has been given to me. Therefore go and make disciples of all nations, baptising them in the name of the Father and of the Son and of the Holy Spirit, and teaching them to obey everything I have commanded you. And surely I am with you always, to the very end of the age.[21]

Here, Jesus himself makes it clear that baptism is only part of what it is to be his disciple. To be baptized into the name of Jesus without also trusting Jesus' words about his staggering authority (which encompasses the entire globe) and continuous presence (through all eternity) makes little sense. These are outrageously egocentric claims – unless they're true. And if they're not true, why would anyone want to be baptized into the name of a liar? Furthermore, Jesus instructed that baptizing people was but the first step in discipleship: 'teaching them to obey everything I have commanded you' was the equally vital next step.

In fact, the jigsaw piece of baptism presupposes that the 'believing' piece is already in place – for a person cannot be baptized unless they trust in Christ. And properly understood, baptism cannot be separated from the 'behaving' piece (for baptism signals death to the old way of life and the beginning of a new life) or the 'belonging' piece (for baptism signals entrance to the family of God). It also ties in very closely with the final piece of the jigsaw, to which we now turn.

Questions for reflection

1. Have you been baptized? Why / why not?

   Read Matthew 28:18–20, Jesus' last recorded words to his disciples.

2. What astonishing claims does Jesus make about his authority, his remit, his teaching and his presence? Do you believe his claims?

3. If you've been baptized, what difference does it make to think about your baptism in the light of these verses?

4. What does it mean to be baptized 'in the name of the Father and of the Son and of the Holy Spirit'? How would you explain it to someone?

   Read Romans 6:1–6.

5. Paul speaks about baptism being a sign of both death and resurrection. If you *have* been baptized, what are some of the things about your pre-Christian life you've had to kill off? What signs of new life are there? If you've *not* been baptized, what are some of the things you would have to kill off?

6. Glance back through the chapter. Talk to God in your own words about something that's challenged or encouraged you.

Piece 5: Born again

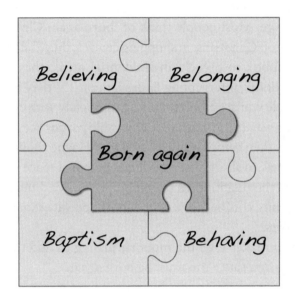

'When I was younger, I remember going to hear Billy Graham at Wembley. At the end, he invited people to be "born again". It was surreal to see so many people going forward, wanting to becoming Christians. I didn't bother going forward, but two people I knew did. For one, it didn't make any difference. The other went a bit overboard with the whole faith-thing afterwards, in my opinion.' (Catherine, sixty-seven)

'I was channel hopping the other day and came across God TV. It was slightly mesmerizing and downright disturbing. There

was this credit-card number rolling across the bottom of the
screen, whilst this preacher told an audience that they "must be
born again". It's fundamentalists like that who really discredit
Christianity. I wish they'd never been born in the first place!'
(Tyler, eighteen)

Let's be up-front about it: 'born-again Christians' don't have a
good image. Most people think of 'born-again Christians' as
over-the-top Christians: in shopping centres, they'll stand up on
their soapbox to preach; in residential areas, they'll knock
on front doors, interrupting *Eastenders*; on TV, they'll claim to
heal people whilst gospel choirs sing smoochily with eyes closed
and arms waving; at otherwise enjoyable parties they'll corner
someone, then launch into a lengthy monologue about society's
ills, and hell. In short, they invade our personal space with their
message, shoving it down people's throats. We'd much prefer
to have a nice cool beer or a mug of hot chocolate slipping down
our throats.

Which makes it all the more surprising to find that it was
Jesus who first said, 'You must be born again.'

Surprise 1: *Jesus* said, 'You must be born again'

It wasn't some fundamentalist American evangelist who said it
first. It was Jesus – the most loving man who's ever lived –
who first coined the phrase.[1] Which makes me think that:

1. being 'born again' doesn't involve soapboxes and gospel
   choirs;
2. we mustn't dismiss the idea of being 'born again' out of
   hand – instead, we need to listen carefully to understand
   exactly what Jesus meant.

Surprise 2: what it *means* to be born again

At the moment, our local rugby club, Bristol, isn't doing too well. Suppose I go along to one of their training sessions to offer my services. 'I've come to help you out,' I say. 'With me on the team, I know you'll move up the table. Please give me a trial.'

After I've pestered them all morning, they eventually invite me in. To start with, they test my general fitness with some running. After sixty seconds, I'm panting. 'It's OK,' I say. 'I'm a bit unfit at the moment, but I'll get back to full fitness in no time.'

Next, they test my ball-handling skills. They throw a series of rugby balls to me, each of which I have to catch and then pass. The first ball I fumble but then pass; the second I catch but then pass atrociously; the third I drop altogether. The exercise comes to an end when the fourth ball hits me on the head and knocks me to the ground.

Finally, they test my physical strength by asking me to tackle other players. At the third attempt, I manage to grab hold of one of the other player's legs to pull him down, but it transpires that he's twice my weight, and he just carries on running anyway. He drags me through the mud for thirty yards before I eventually let go.

At the end of the trial, I go up to the coach and say, 'So how about it? I know I need to work on one or two areas, but can you see my potential? Will you take me on?' He cocks one eyebrow at me, starts walking away and calls over his shoulder, 'Frankly, mate, I wouldn't take you unless you were born again. You'll never be a rugby player. Stick to tiddlywinks.'

His message to me is clear, isn't it? Given my body and skills, I haven't a hope. No amount of practice and coaching will ever make a sufficient difference. I'm just not cut out for rugby.

So when Jesus said, 'I tell you the truth, no-one can see the kingdom of God unless he is born again,'[2] he was saying that no amount of practice and coaching will get someone into God's kingdom. By ourselves, we're simply not cut out for it. We need a completely new start.

So to be 'born again' isn't to become fanatical about religion; it's to wipe away all religion and have a new start. When Jesus says, 'You must be born again,'[3] he's not saying, 'I want you to try harder: turn over a new leaf.' He's saying, 'You need a new life.' It's a deeply surprising message.

'I tell you the truth,' Jesus carried on. 'No-one can see the kingdom of God without being born of water and the Spirit. Flesh gives birth to flesh, but the Spirit gives birth to spirit.'[4] In other words, Jesus isn't talking about a *physical* re-birth, but a *spiritual* birth. If someone has only been born of a human mother, they are but flesh. It's not until someone is born of the heavenly Father *as well* that they become spiritually alive.

At Christmas carol services, the opening of John's Gospel is almost always read. Talking about Jesus, it says, 'To those who believed in his name, he gave the right to become children of God – children born not of natural descent, nor of human decision or a husband's will, but born of God.' We could put it like this: Jesus was physically born of Mary so that people could be spiritually born of God.

Surprise 3: *who* Jesus was talking to

Let's backtrack a bit. When Jesus said, 'You must be born again,' he was actually talking with a chap called Nicodemus. He's introduced to us as 'a Pharisee . . . a member of the Jewish ruling council'.[5] In other words, he was very religious indeed, and highly respected. In today's terms, he was a cross between a bishop, an MP and a professor of theology.

But it wasn't just his *status* that was impressive: his *character* was impressive as well. He was a very nice man. A very, very nice man. He was honest, he was concerned for the poor, he gave to charity. He dressed smartly, he had high moral principles, he longed for a better society. He took his religion seriously, too: he read his Scriptures avidly, prayed fervently and went to services regularly. You would be hard-pressed to find a single bad thing to say about him.

So when Jesus said to him, '*You* must be born again,' we should be surprised. Very surprised. Surely if *anyone* was going to get into God's kingdom, Nicodemus would. Didn't he do everything God wanted him to do? Think of the jigsaw. He *believed* fervently in God. He *behaved* impeccably – he would have been able to recite all the laws off by heart, so concerned was he to keep them. He *belonged* to the Old Testament equivalent of the church – in fact, he didn't just belong to it, he helped lead it! And although he hadn't been *baptized*, he had

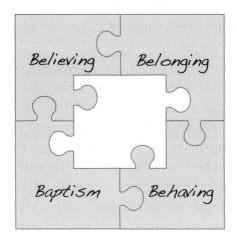

been circumcised – God's prescribed Old Testament membership sign for Jews.

Can you see? Nicodemus had four pieces of the jigsaw in
place, but still Jesus said he needed something more: to be born
again.

We should be somewhat concerned by Jesus telling Nicodemus
he needed to be born again, because if Jesus said that to such a
decent, law-abiding, religious chap, who else would he say it to?
We can be sure Jesus didn't just mean that *Nicodemus* needed
to be born again, for the word he uses for 'you' is plural. In fact,
by saying this to the most religious and respectable of people,
Jesus was making his point very clearly: *no-one* can enter the
kingdom of God unless they are born again. Not Nicodemus.
Not the Pope. Not Rick Warren. Not Mother Teresa. Not the
Archbishop of Canterbury. Not me. Not you. There are no
exceptions.

Each one of us needs a miracle to enter God's kingdom,
including me. None of us drift in. None of us gain automatic
entry. None of us get welcomed in by our own effort. None of
us have a short-cut because of who we know. None of us get
waved in because of who we are. Jesus says that there is only
one way to enter God's kingdom: to be born again.

'But why?' you ask.

Do you remember what we said when we looked at 'belief'
– that God is holy (perfect) and that we are sinful (imperfect)?
Even Nicodemus would have admitted that – he knew his own
shortcomings. But what he hadn't appreciated was how deep-
seated his problem was. His problem (and ours, if we're honest)
wasn't just that he was sinful, but that he couldn't stop being
sinful. That's why, however hard we try, we still land up hurting
those we love most – our words or actions just come out wrong.
That's why, however hard we try, we still end up getting on each

other's nerves in the office. That's why, however hard we try, we cannot help being secretly jealous of those who have more than us. That's why, however hard we try, families continue to have arguments.

We think that we're like perfectly formed round balls. Given a chance, we will roll in a straight line on the ground. If we go off course, we blame it on the slope. God says that in reality we're like those weighted balls that children throw in the air, which wobble uncontrollably and fall unpredictably. Or we're like the slightly asymmetric bowls used in lawn bowls: we're always veering to the side; we're incapable of going straight. And it's no-one's fault but our own.

Just as I'm not cut out for rugby – I'd ruin the team! – so none of us are cut out for the kingdom of God (his perfect kingdom) – we'd ruin it. Even Nicodemus would ruin it. That's why we need a miracle – we need to be born again.

To describe someone as a 'born-again Christian' is a bit like talking about a 'two-wheeled bicycle'. Every bicycle has two wheels by definition! Similarly, Jesus is saying that every genuine Christian has been born again; it's impossible to be part of his kingdom without it.

Surprise 4: *how* the second birth happens

Jesus gave Nicodemus a quick history lesson next. If you're like me, and didn't really get on with history at school, don't panic: it's only a quick lesson. Jesus reminded Nicodemus of a strange incident in Israel's history when the people were wandering through the desert, complaining at God and Moses about their lack of food and water.[6] What happened next reminded them equally of God's power to judge and his power to save. Poisonous snakes started giving fatal bites to the Israelites; many died. After a while, they realized their mistake in complaining to God, so they repented, and asked God to rescue them from the snakes. God instructed Moses to make a bronze snake, and lift it up high, and told him that if anyone had been bitten, they merely had to look at the bronze snake to be cured. Sure enough, those who'd been bitten looked at the snake and lived.

Jesus doesn't let Nicodemus be distracted by how the cure worked. The important thing, he says, is the *pattern* – which was about to be replicated. 'Just as Moses lifted up the snake in the desert, so the Son of Man [Jesus himself] must be lifted up, that everyone who believes in him may have eternal life.'[7] Jesus was anticipating his death, when he would be lifted up on the cross. Just as the dying Israelites who looked to Moses' bronze snake were cured, so also those who look to Jesus' death on the cross will be rescued.

Here's the important thing: the Israelites who'd been bitten knew that their injuries would prove fatal, and that they had no hope of survival other than trusting in God's provision. So it is with us. These are the pre-conditions under which God's Spirit is able to bring someone to new birth. We must recognize that:

- by ourselves, we have no hope of entry into God's kingdom (we're just not cut out for it – we need to be born again);
- our only hope of entry to God's kingdom is if he provides a way – which he has by Jesus' death.

Surprise 5: the *effect* it has

By now, maybe you're thinking that all this sounds incredibly other-worldly. But it works!

Real lives - Tom

Tom, thirty-one, is a software engineer, cricketer and LeRoc dancer.

I'd been brought up as a Roman Catholic, but stopped going to church when I was about thirteen. Years later, I decided to go to a church – the only one I could find that put its times on the Internet. I went on an Alpha course, and enjoyed the discussions. A few weeks later, at a communion service, the vicar said, 'Jesus is here with us.' All of a sudden I was certain that he was. At that moment I knew I had to make a decision either to accept the love of Jesus and the gift of his sacrifice, abandoning my pride in my intellectual ability – or else reject him forever. It was a stark choice. In those few moments I decided to lay down my pride, open the door to Jesus and take a small step towards him in faith, so I got up and received communion. *That* was the moment at which I gave myself to Jesus just a little bit.

Suddenly everything was different. Later that day, rather than standing with my arms folded whilst everyone else was singing, I found that not only was I singing, but singing with great joy, and there were tears flowing. I realized that *all* I wanted to do was sing praises and worship God, in pure joy and gratitude for what he has done for us.

Over the next few days I exchanged a series of emails with my Mum that made me realize that my relationship with her had been badly broken for fourteen years, and that she knew this, whereas I had no idea.

It was as if, when I opened the door to Jesus just a little bit, there was a wall of water outside ready to rush in and fill every little part of my life, cleaning it out. I've been blown away by the power of Jesus to change my life.

What Tom had found, along with millions of others, is that the simple act of submitting to God in repentance and faith paves the way for God's Spirit to work a miracle in us: to make us born again. Because Tom was humble enough to lay down his pride and open the door to Jesus, all of a sudden, Tom was cut out for the kingdom of God, and his relationship with God and his family began to be transformed.

Three days ago, we had deep snow – enough to close the schools. Two days ago, we had heavy rain – enough to cause flooding. Last night, we had strong winds – enough to blow the neighbour's fence down, and keep me awake. I have a lot of sympathy for those who choose to emigrate to Mediterranean climates!

We've all seen the powerful *effects* of wind – fallen trees, fluttering flags, gliding windsurfers. But which of us have *seen* the wind itself or can predict where it will blow next? None of us. The reason for mentioning all this is that Jesus likens the powerful wind to God's powerful Spirit (in the original Bible languages, the same word is translated either as 'wind' or 'spirit'). 'The wind blows wherever it pleases,' said Jesus. 'You hear its sound, but you cannot tell where it comes from or where it is going. So it is with everyone born of the Spirit.'[8] He's saying that none of us can predict in whom God's Spirit will work next, and none of us should be surprised by how powerful his work is.

I've just heard the story of a teenager who became a Christian in the back of a funeral car on the way to his best friend's funeral.

I remember reading the story of someone who became a Christian just as they were planning to throw a bomb into a church gathering. I recall the story of a Hindu who thought he was going to a business meeting, but ended up in a church meeting, captivated by the message of the gospel. Yesterday, I read of an undergraduate, a staunch atheist, who went to some Christian meetings and became convinced by the truth of Jesus. No-one could have predicted that those people were about to become Christians: but that is how God's Spirit works – he blows wherever he pleases.

And the transformation that Tom began to experience as a result of the Spirit's work in his life is just a *glimpse* of the quality of life that Jesus wants us to enjoy. As Jesus said next, 'For God so loved the world that he gave his one and only Son, that whoever believes in him shall not perish but have *eternal life.'*[9] Elsewhere, Jesus calls such life 'life to the full'[10] and makes it clear that such life doesn't kick in when we kick the bucket; it starts *now*.

It's the sort of life where relationships are restored, forgiveness becomes possible, arguments lessen, bitterness evaporates. It's the sort of life where we can know peace in the midst of a crisis,[11] contentment in spite of severe deprivation,[12] hope instead of despair,[13] delight despite weaknesses.[14] It's the sort of life where, having been born into God's family, we begin to get to know God as an intimate Father[15] – 'Papa' – rather than as a distant Almighty God; and where we discover Jesus calls us his friend, rather than his servant.[16] Being born again makes all the difference in the world.

The changes aren't necessarily instantaneous. There may be some things that change overnight, but other aspects of the transformation take a lifetime. Slowly but surely, our heavenly Father wants us to know and experience a wholeness to life that includes the healing of the deep emotional scars which have wounded and disabled so many people.

How does this jigsaw piece fit with all the others?

Last Christmas, my brother gave us a jigsaw with a difference. It was a specially printed jigsaw of an aerial picture of our house and the surrounding area. It was fascinating to see how our local area 'fitted together' from a bird's-eye perspective – and very useful for continuing to learn our way round this new area!

We did what you always do with jigsaws – start with the outside and work in. It was only as we got near the end that we discovered that the very central piece was of our house – and that this one piece was even shaped like a house.

Throughout this book, I've pictured Jesus' definition of a Christian as being like a jigsaw with several different pieces. There's something special about this final piece, which is why I've put it in the middle.

Like all the other pieces, it's insufficient by itself. There are a few people who say they were born again years ago, but clearly very few of the other pieces of the jigsaw have ever been put in place: they don't go to church regularly, and their lives haven't been transformed. To be honest, that's a sign they never fully appreciated that they were being born again *into God's family* (*belonging* to the church), and that by being born into God's family, God now wanted to begin forming the family likeness (*behaving* like Jesus) in them. For those people, the picture as a whole is still a bit of a mess and incomplete.

But I suspect there are far more people like Nicodemus: people who've got lots of the other pieces in place, but are missing this one.

One writer compares many people's experience of being a Christian to being in a swimming pool or pond:

> Many Christians are unaware that there is a deep end. They have become so used to living in the shallows that they think this is the norm. Perhaps this is not all they expected when they first found themselves in the pond, but they are generally content to paddle until they get to the big pond in the sky. Occasionally they hear rumours that there is a deep end, they meet the odd person who claims to have come from the deep end, one or two of the fellow shallow-enders have even left them and said they are off to the deep end and every now and again they wonder, 'So, how do I get to this deep end?'[17]

Maybe that describes you. For you, your experience of being a Christian is more one of duty than joy. Your experience of prayer is all too often of formulaic words, rather than of a conversation. Your experience of church services is one of slight detachment – letting it all wash over you – rather than genuine engagement. You're paddling in the shallows. How do you get to the deep end?

Billy Graham, the most famous Christian leader of the twentieth century, said,

> Everywhere I go I find that God's people lack something. They are hungry for something. Their Christian experience is not all that they expected and they often have recurring defeat in their lives. Christians today are hungry for spiritual fulfilment. The most desperate need of the nation today is that men and women who profess Jesus be filled with the Holy Spirit.[18]

Real lives - Ken

This story is a bit different – I took Ken's funeral a couple of years ago. His son tells his story:

Dad grew up going to church regularly, and was confirmed as a teenager. After the war, he had an active social life, but continued to go to church from time to time. After he got married and I was born, my parents went to church regularly, partly so I could go to Sunday school.

Soon after Dad retired, my parents were invited along to a Saturday morning breakfast with a Christian speaker, who talked about his experience of God. They went along to the church regularly, and after a year or two, he acknowledged that there was something about the people there that, even though he'd gone to church more or less all his life, he was missing. Eventually he went up for prayer, and knew he'd been born again at that point.

He'd read his Bible before then, but after that experience, it became much more real to him, and was an important means by which his relationship with God developed.

Dad's was a very personal, emotional faith. What was important to him was his experience of the Holy Spirit in worship and the encouragement of seeing God at work in his life and in the lives of his fellow Christians. Knowing Jesus as his Lord sustained him as he faced the challenges of the last twenty years of his life. His faith gave him a cheerfulness and peace that he would not otherwise have had. He died secure in his knowledge of Christ, and confident of his hope of heaven.

Two things make this piece of the jigsaw so special. First, someone can make a good *pretence* of having all the other pieces in place by simple outward actions: they can be baptized, go to church, recite the creed and live a good life – all without really meaning it. But this is the only piece that can't easily be forged, because it touches our hearts, the core of our being. Being born again leaves no room for pride, because we have to confess our absolute helplessness apart from God. And being born again takes humility, because it's an invitation for God's Spirit to transform us from within. It's only as God's Spirit is at work in our hearts that we can experience the joy, fulfilment and peace that God longs for us to know.

Second, this piece of the jigsaw is special because being born again by the Holy Spirit brings all the other pieces to life:

- What used to be a dry *belief* in God becomes a personal *trust* in God – an expectation that God can and will work in very personal ways in our lives.
- What used to be a dutiful attendance at a church becomes a genuine *belonging* – an excitement about being part of a close-knit group where we can use our Spirit-given gifts to serve others.
- What used to be a somewhat begrudging observance of God's laws (or at least, of those laws we agreed with) becomes a deep-seated desire to *behave* in a way that pleases our loving heavenly Father, aided by God's Spirit giving us power to change as he forms the fruit of the Spirit in us.
- What was, in an infant *baptism*, felt to be some sort of magic naming ceremony with water, becomes a wonderful sign of having been washed clean by God, something so desperately needed.

On the quiz show *A Question of Sport*, they sometimes show a sports personality with their face blanked out. You can still see some of their hair or ears or hands, but you can't see the central face. It's very difficult to work out who the hair and ears and hands belong to! But as soon as the face itself is revealed, it all becomes clear and makes sense. So it is with this jigsaw. The four pieces round the edge are recognizable as somehow part of being a Christian, but with the central piece missing, none of it really makes sense. It simply doesn't work.

The essential spiritual experience

You've probably heard horror stories of people who've set off on holiday, only to get to the airport and realize they've forgotten their passport. As they quickly find out, you can't get anywhere without one – they're essential!

Jesus didn't say that to get into God's kingdom, we *may* be born again. He said we *must* be born again – it's essential! Let me repeat what I said at the beginning. Being born again isn't anything to do with waving hands in the air at church or pestering others about their lack of faith. But nor is being born again an optional extra for the very keen Christian. It's one of the distinguishing marks of every Christian. If you haven't been born again, you're not a genuine Christian, and you're not a part of God's kingdom.

Some people ask, 'I can't remember being born again. Does that mean I haven't been born again?' In fact, I'm in that group. I grew up going to church and learning about Jesus. I never had a time when I significantly turned away from Jesus or his church. As I look back, I can see particular periods of growth in my faith and understanding of being a Christian, but I can't remember being born again. Does that mean I haven't been born again?

Not necessarily. After all, none of us can remember being born, and none of us would know when we were born if our parents hadn't told us. What matters is whether we have been born again. Have we had that sense of awful realization that by ourselves we are not worthy to enter God's kingdom, coupled with an utter reliance on Jesus' death as our passport in? In doing so, have you opened yourself up to the wind of God's Spirit blowing through your life to change you from the inside out? In my case, the answer's 'yes'. Is it for you?

Other people say, 'I'm a Christian because I was born in this country.' Jesus says, 'It's not *where* you were born that makes you a Christian, it's *how many times* you've been born. A Christian is someone who's been born again.'

Some people say, 'I'm a Christian because I was brought up in a Christian home.' Jesus replies, 'It doesn't matter if you were born to believing *parents*. What matters is if you *yourself* have been born again – born of God.'

Still others say, 'I'm a pillar of our church and community.' Jesus says, 'Yes, so was Nicodemus. But as I told him, so I tell you: *no-one* can see the kingdom of God unless they are born again.'

What would Jesus say to you? Would he reassure you that this piece is firmly in place – or would he tell you that it's missing?

Questions for reflection

1. Imagine this is a scale of goodness, with God at the top.

100 – perfectly good – GOD

0 – horribly bad

Where on the scale would you plot Adolf Hitler? Widely respected Christians like Mother Teresa and Billy Graham have been painfully aware of their own shortcomings. Where would you plot them? Where would you plot yourself?

2. Look at the gap between where you are and where God is. Can you see what Jesus means when he says that we're not cut out for God's kingdom – that we need to be born again?

Turn to John 3, the account of Jesus' conversation with Nicodemus.

3. Read verses 1–2. What does Nicodemus make of Jesus? In what way did he underestimate Jesus (see verses 12–13)?
4. Read verses 3–8. What did Jesus make of Nicodemus? In what ways had Nicodemus overestimated himself? Might you have overestimated yourself?
5. Read Ezekiel 36:25–27 – an ancient prophecy that was in the back of Jesus' mind as he spoke to Nicodemus. It talks of new life coming by water and Spirit. Do you think you've had the sort of heart surgery performed on you by God that the prophet talks about?
6. Glance back through the chapter. Talk to God in your own words about something that's challenged or encouraged you.

Conclusion:
Putting the pieces together

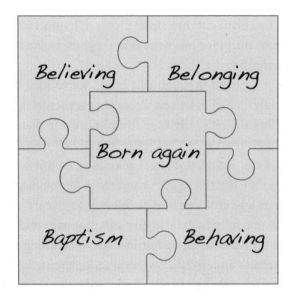

'I grew up in Northern Ireland – you can't get away from religion there. I moved to Scotland to go to uni. A friend said to me the other day, "There are no Catholics or Protestants, only Christians and non-Christians." I dismissed it at first, but it's got under my skin. He's right: surely the two religions both believe in Jesus and God? I know which religion I am, but to be honest, I'm not sure if I'm a Christian.' (Fiona, twenty-three)

'My wife takes the kids to church most weeks, and I go along sometimes. It's a good family thing to do together, and I'm pleased the kids are being taught right and wrong. For myself, there's something calming about church. It makes a nice change from work, at least. So I suppose I'm a Christian, although I've never really thought about it.' (Martin, forty-seven)

Recently I read the story of a binman who found £10,000 in notes crammed into two litter bins. Unfortunately for him, all the notes had been cut into small pieces. He now faces a painstaking jigsaw puzzle to piece the notes together – but his reward if he completes it is £10,000!

As we've worked through this book, we've seen how Jesus says five different things need to come together in the life of a genuine Christian. It's only as all five pieces are in place that you or I can have assurance that Jesus would call us a Christian. You would think that is doesn't take long to put a five-piece jigsaw together. But the jigsaw described in this book takes some people years and even decades to finish. A few years ago, I took the funeral of a friend who'd been christened as a child, searched spiritually for most of her adult life, started coming to church in her seventies and eventually became a genuine Christian in her eighties, shortly before she died.

I can remember doing a large jigsaw with some friends late one evening. Several times I looked at my watch and thought, 'I'll just do five more minutes, then go to bed.' But jigsaws are so addictive! I'd keep spotting where another piece might fit. In the end, the jigsaw neared completion in the small hours, but as we put the final pieces in, it became obvious there was a piece missing. Can you imagine how frustrated we felt? Of course, we didn't just shrug our shoulders and say 'Good night' to one another. There was no satisfaction until, having searched high and low for the missing piece, we found it.

Sadly, many people never complete the jigsaw that makes up Jesus' definition of a Christian. They have a few of the pieces in place, but others are missing – and they don't go in search of them.

That's such a shame, because the reward for completing the jigsaw is infinitely more than the simple satisfaction of a job well done. In fact, it's infinitely more even than £10,000. The reward for completing this jigsaw is what Jesus describes as 'eternal life', 'life to the full', 'seeing the kingdom of God'. It's to live life as we were made to live it. Anyone who hasn't finished this jigsaw is selling themselves short, paddling in the shallows.

Finding the missing piece

Consider the following:

> *Jim was invited along to a church by a friend, and has found it to be a really welcoming community. He's become a regular member, and will often be found doing practical jobs around the church with others. Over a number of months, Jim's views about God have gradually been getting clearer. He's started praying short prayers at home, and feels good about that. He's stopped swearing so much as well.*

Which pieces of the jigsaw has Jim got? It's clear that it's a developing picture. He clearly belongs to the church, and his belief is growing. His behaviour is starting to change. It's not completely clear whether Jim has been born again yet – maybe he'd find it helpful to ask his pastor to outline the core of the Christian faith, and if he's happy with that, to pray some sort of prayer of commitment to God with him, to help him confirm the direction he's moving in. If he does that, he'll probably want to get baptized as well.

> Asha was converted in her twenties, having been to an Alpha course at a church with a large congregation. Over the course of a few months, she became convinced that Jesus was who he said he was, and that he died to forgive her. She committed her life to him, and was baptized. However, the church seems to have quite a conservative stance on some ethical issues – something she struggles with, because she's got gay friends, and has been sleeping with her Christian boyfriend for ages. In fact, she had an abortion a few months ago. She can tell she's starting to keep God at arm's length.

What a great start Asha made! Most of the pieces seem to have been put in place very quickly. The piece that's missing is the 'behaving' piece. Maybe she didn't realize when she became a Christian that Jesus would want to change her lifestyle over time. She might find it helpful to talk and pray with one of the women on the pastoral team at her church. If Asha says that she loves Jesus and that he's her Lord, then she needs to let him shape her thinking and acting. It'll be painful at times – especially when talking about the abortion – but she'll discover more of God's goodness and grace as she works through these issues.

> Geoffrey was baptized as a baby and confirmed at thirteen. He takes great pride in having been part of St Mary's for over forty years and has done everything: work-parties, reading the lesson, organizing the socials, counting the collection, delivering the parish magazine, etc. On the whole, he lives a pretty decent life. There have been a few times when he's made confession to his priest, but he still feels a bit guilty for those lapses. He hasn't been too keen on some of the services the new priest has initiated for children.

On the surface, Geoffrey looks very impressive! But there's no mention of his belief. He probably says the creed week by week, but would he be able to explain his belief in his own words? Does he pray by himself? Is he seeking *God's* will for the church, or does he just want things to stay as they are for his *own* sake? And I wonder if he's actually been born again: if we asked him why God should let him into heaven, would he say it's because of his church credentials, or would he say that he's not worthy to get into heaven – he's simply trusting in Jesus' death?

Kate's got a husband, three teenage children and a full-time job which takes her away from home at least once a week. She also goes to the gym twice a week. She's always had a strong belief in God. She was baptized as a baby and grew up going to Sunday school. Her faith is very important to her – she prays daily, and asks Jesus for forgiveness. She makes sure the family goes to church at Christmas and Easter, but she's simply too busy to go regularly.

Again, Kate has several pieces of the jigsaw in place: baptism, belief and behaviour. But at the moment, her family, career and leisure pursuits are squeezing her faith out. Sad to say, she will find it harder and harder over time to keep her faith alive without the love and support of a church family. Would she have the strength to resist if a work contact propositioned her regularly on those business trips? Besides, how will her husband and children come to faith in Christ, if they have such irregular contact with the church? Something's got to give. If God is really going to be the centre of her life, she needs to give some other things up, and become an active part of God's family.

Jon grew up going to church, and loved it. The best thing was the summer activity camps. At one of these, he was really struck by a talk

*explaining why Jesus died, and he prayed a prayer of commitment.
He started reading his Bible regularly, but when he went to university,
he never got round to church. He's been working for a couple of years
now in a graduate job, and living with his girlfriend. He still believes
in Jesus and goes to church when he's visiting his parents. But he
thinks Christianity is simply unrealistic in the real world of twenty-
first-century business and relationships.*

The world is Jon's oyster. He's living life as he chooses, so his
belonging and behaving pieces simply aren't there at the moment.
Maybe he's never understood that Jesus didn't come to cramp his
style, but to enable him to live life to the full! Perhaps Jon and
his girlfriend should find a church with other people their age,
and watch how those friends live out their Christian lives. Going
on a Christianity Explored or Alpha course[1] might serve as a
refresher for Jon. Above all, he needs to know that he's got nothing
to lose by reconsidering his Christian faith, and everything to gain.

*Helen went forward at a Billy Graham rally as a teenager. She got
baptized a few months later and was really keen in her faith for at
least ten years. After a while, her marriage broke up. She still goes to
church quite often, but now she deliberately sits on the edge. She tries
her best to live a good life, but doesn't find it easy. If she's honest, she
isn't sure what she believes about God any more.*

Helen's jigsaw picture seems to have been much clearer before
the pain of her divorce. The pieces labelled 'born again' and
'baptized' are still in place, but the 'believing', 'belonging'
and 'behaving' pieces are faded or missing. Maybe Helen would
find it helpful to go on a Christianity Explored or Alpha course
– they can be very helpful for those wanting to work out what
they believe about God. That sort of environment would also

help her get to know others in the church better. She would probably find that 'behaving' (living as Jesus wants her to) gets easier as she makes time to think through what she believes and gets more involved in the church.

> Anthony was converted as a teenager, and used to be really involved in the church. He played in the music group and led some Bible studies in one of the small groups. But as he got more involved and looked behind the scenes at the church, he didn't like what he saw. Things came to a head, and there was a very painful split in the church. Anthony stopped going altogether. He still believes in God, and prays and reads Bible stories to his children, but he's afraid of joining a church again – for fear of getting hurt.

Anthony's got lots of the jigsaw pieces in place, but is understandably hurt and fearful after his horrible experience with his former church. However, as time goes on, Anthony will actually find it increasingly difficult to keep up his Christian faith by himself. God has wired us up in such a way that belonging to a church strengthens our belief when we doubt (how would Anthony cope – spiritually and practically – if one of his children was taken seriously ill?), and also spurs us on to behave as Jesus wants us to. Anthony may need to find another church and meet up with their minister to work through his previous experiences.

The myth of the 'incomplete Christian'

The people described above are all fictional, but not uncommon. I wonder if you can identify with any of them.

A few of those people might say, 'I think I'm a Christian.' But as someone once said to me, 'If you only *think* you're a

Christian, it probably means you're *not* a Christian.' After all, if someone could only say, 'I *think* I'm a Tory' or 'I *think* I'm Labour', it would almost certainly indicate that they're not fully signed up party members, even if their political leanings are in that direction. Jesus wants us to be *sure* we're a Christian (not just lean in that direction), and that assurance comes as we see all the boxes ticked, all the pieces in place.

Of course, for some of the pieces, there's always more that could be done: our belief in God could be stronger, our behaviour could be more Christ-like, our commitment to the church could be deeper. Jesus doesn't necessarily expect perfection in these areas, but he does at least want the pieces to be clearly visible: clinging to belief, even as we doubt; giving ourselves to the church, even when it's hard work; desiring God's forgiveness and help to be more Christ-like, even when we slip up.

Most of the people described above would probably say, 'I *am* a Christian.' But remember: the important question isn't whether they call *themselves* a 'Christian', it's whether *Jesus* would call them a Christian. None of these people seems to have all the pieces of this jigsaw clearly in place. So maybe when Jesus returns to judge each one of us, they would be among the many people who say, 'Lord, Lord, did we not . . . [serve you]?', to whom Jesus will reply, 'I never knew you. Away from me, you evildoers!' It sounds very harsh even to suggest that. But we have to take Jesus' warning seriously: 'Not every-one who says to me, "Lord, Lord" will enter the kingdom of heaven.'[2]

Please hear me clearly on this: it's not my place to be judge and jury. I'm not trying to cast judgment on anyone. I'm simply trying to help us work out what *Jesus* – who *will* be our judge one day – will say to us. We would be foolish to *assume* his warning isn't directed at us.

Real lives - Jonny

Jonny, forty-four, is a vicar, father of four, and a keen sportsman.

I went to Mass at least once a week with my family until my parents separated. When I was eighteen, I moved in with my elder brother. Out of boredom and wanting to meet some nice girls, I went along to his church youth group. What really made an impression on me was how uncommonly friendly everyone was. We got into lots of discussions about God and the Christian life. I considered myself a Christian, but I thought these guys were just too keen. It changed how they lived. They needed to chill out a bit – or so I thought.

Things radically changed for me when I started reading Matthew's Gospel. I was familiar with all the stories, but then I read Jesus saying, 'That is how it will be at the coming of the Son of Man. Two men will be in the field; one will be taken and the other left. Two women will be grinding with a hand mill; one will be taken and the other left. Therefore keep watch, because you do not know on what day your Lord will come.'[3] This was like dynamite. As I lay in bed, I looked over at my brother and thought. 'If Jesus came tonight, he would be taken and I would be left behind.' Shortly after that, I committed my life to following Jesus whatever the cost.

I've realized that the Christian faith isn't about being good in my own eyes, but being acceptable in God's eyes. It's about a God-centred world, not a me-centred world.

I always wanted to do something with my life that I thought I could pour my heart and soul into. But before I became a Christian I didn't really know what. Following Jesus gave me the answer. The penny dropped when someone challenged me to go into full-time Christian ministry. There's nothing I'd rather do than spend my life telling people about Jesus and all he's done for us.

Right from the earliest days of the church, it's clear that there have been some who *think* they're part of God's kingdom, but then discover they're wrong:

- In Acts 10, we read about a Roman centurion, Cornelius, who was 'devout and God-fearing; he gave generously to those in need and prayed to God regularly'.[4] Through a series of dreams and visions, the apostle Peter was sent to him and his family to re-affirm what they already knew about Jesus, that through his death he had come to bring forgiveness of sins. It was only at this point that the message became personal to them: the family were born again, filled with God's Spirit, and subsequently baptized.

- In Galatians, we discover that the believers there had started really well – they were 'running a good race'.[5] They'd been genuinely converted. But now, under the influence of some false teachers, they were no longer trusting in Jesus' death for their forgiveness. Significantly, their change in belief meant that they had lost their joy[6] – for now they thought they had to work hard to maintain their salvation. On hearing this news, the apostle Paul wrote his sternest letter, saying they'd 'fallen away from grace' and were now 'alienated from Christ'.[7] He begs them to return to the gospel of grace.

- In the book of Revelation, Jesus says to people at a church in Sardis, 'Wake up! Strengthen what remains and is about to die, for I have not found your deeds complete in the sight of my God . . . if you do not wake up, I will come like a thief, and you will not know at what time I will come to you.'[8]

Here's the important thing: in none of these cases were the 'believers' patted on the back and told 'you're doing well as a Christian'. In each case, they were implored to finish the jigsaw puzzle. Cornelius had never had some of the pieces, but quickly put them in place. The 'Christians' in Galatia and Sardis used to have a complete picture, but it was now badly broken up and needed to be put back together again.

Real lives - Anna

Anna, twenty-eight, is a teacher who's counting down the days to her wedding.

When I was eleven, my father left my mother. We stopped attending church regularly, and I remember feeling God had let me down. As the years progressed, my mother began to try to rebuild her relationship with God. Over time, a penny dropped for her and she became comfortable again in her faith. She seemed so much calmer and at peace with herself. My stepfather took the Alpha course and he also began to display the same signs of serenity and unshakeable confidence in his faith. I became intrigued.

When I was asked by a friend to become a godmother, I felt I had to explore fully my relationship with God before taking those vows. My belief in God was helped by attending a church regularly, but I felt very distant from other members of the congregation. I had so many questions. I remember sitting in church many times, being unable to feel what those around me seemed to be feeling. I wanted to know why, if God was this wonderful Father, he could allow so much hurt and pain to happen. I also wondered how I would ever be able to live a completely sin-free life. I would ask God to help me fully believe and to take away my doubts and answer my questions, but it seemed slow in coming.

At a Christianity Explored course, for the first time I had the confidence to air my doubts. I asked loads of awkward questions. I slowly realized that being a Christian isn't about knowing all the answers, but about putting your faith in God. I also realized that I will never be sin-free and that the fantastic news is that Jesus died for my sin and that God loves me in spite of it.

The thing that has surprised me most about being a Christian is the amazing feeling of having someone by my side. I've also been shocked by the power of prayer and the lovely feeling that comes from belonging to a church family.

At our church, I help lead a course for anyone who wants to explore the basics of the Christian faith. Quite a few of the guests who come have a church background of some sort. They describe themselves as Christians, but with lots of questions and doubts. It's not unusual for these people to realize after a few weeks that, although they think of themselves as Christians, maybe Jesus doesn't. That realization is painful – but paves the way for the wonderful experience of becoming a genuine Christian as the course progresses.

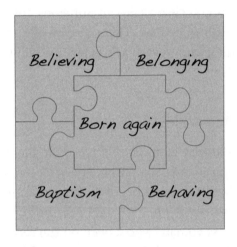

Think for a moment: how many pieces of the jigsaw do you have in place right now? If the answer is one, two, three or four, you've made a good start. But don't stop now – the jigsaw's not finished yet!

Some people describe themselves as 'sort-of Christians' or 'semi-Christian'. Maybe you've come to realize that you haven't got all the pieces in place, so you would describe yourself as an 'incomplete Christian'.

Much as I'd love it if Jesus had a half-way category like that, I'm convinced he doesn't. When he pictured his coming judgment as being like a dairy farmer separating his animals, Jesus didn't talk about *three* groups – the sheep, the goats and the cross-breeds. He just spoke about the sheep and the goats.[9] When God gave the apostle John a glimpse of how Jesus will make his judgment, he saw the book of life – a book containing the names of genuine Christians. Those whose names *were* written in the book entered the new creation; those whose names *weren't* written in the book were 'thrown into the lake of fire'.[10] There was no *third* group.

Jesus makes it as clear as he can: someone either *is* a Christian or they're *not* a Christian. There is no middle ground. There is no such thing as a 'sort-of Christian' or 'half-Christian' or 'incomplete Christian'.

Finishing the puzzle

Shortly after Barack Obama was elected as President of the USA, he was phoning round people who'd been elected to Congress to congratulate them and begin getting to know them. He phoned one, and said, 'Hi, it's Barack Obama here.'

The congresswoman (who'd been on the receiving end of prank calls before) replied, 'You know, you're a better impersonator than that guy who does Obama on *Saturday Night Live*. But I don't believe you.' And she hung up on him.

Can you imagine hanging up on the President of the USA?!

Obama called again, and said, 'How can I convince you that this is Barack?'

The congresswoman wasn't going to be fooled. 'Yeah, sure,' she said. 'Have a nice day.' And she hung up, again.

In the end, other senior politicians had to call her to tell her it really was Barack Obama trying to speak to her, after which she phoned his office and said, 'I know this sounds very presumptuous, but please tell President Obama he can call me now and I will take his call.'

Can you imagine hanging up on the President of the USA?[11] More to the point, can you imagine hanging up on the God of the universe? I fear that is what many people do. They hear God trying to get through to them, but they don't really believe it's God, so they put the phone down again. Or they hear what God is saying, but they're frightened to do what he says. Or they hear the phone ringing, but they don't even pick it up to answer.

Maybe as you've read this book, you've realized that although *you* may call yourself a Christian, *Jesus* wouldn't. Perhaps you didn't know that some of the missing pieces of the jigsaw even existed, or you thought they were optional extras rather than essential pieces. Maybe, if you're honest, you know that God has been on your case for months or even years, but you've been ignoring him. Whatever your story, the important thing to know is that Jesus isn't phoning to condemn you (as if to say, 'You're not a Christian, so I never want to speak to you again!'). Not at all! 'For God did not send his Son into the world to condemn the world, but to save the world through him.'[12] It's as if Jesus is phoning to say, 'Come on, shall we put these missing pieces in place?'

How about it?

Of course, there weren't phones in Jesus' day, but he did use a similar image. Writing to people who *thought* they were Christians,[13] Jesus said, 'I stand at the door and knock.' He was waiting for an answer. He'd already made it very clear to them that they weren't Christians, when he said, 'I am about to spit you out of my mouth.' I think they got the message! Maybe they'd started the jigsaw well, but they hadn't finished it, or some of the pieces had disappeared over time. Whatever the reason, they'd ended up thinking they had no need of Jesus' rescue. They said, 'I do not need a thing.'

But Jesus knows that we all need him. So he said to them, 'You do not realise that you are wretched, pitiful, poor, blind and naked. I counsel you to buy from me gold refined in the fire, so that you can become rich; and white clothes to wear, so that you can cover your shameful nakedness; and salve to put on your eyes, so that you can see.' Can you see that Jesus doesn't *force* himself into people's lives, and that he wants to give what's *good* for us?

He carried on, 'Those whom I love I rebuke and discipline.' Can you see that Jesus' motivation in speaking these harsh words is *love*? We've nothing to fear from someone who loves us so much that he died for us!

'So be earnest,' said Jesus, 'and repent.' That's his command to us, too: to seek his forgiveness for not relying on him and obeying him, and to take action to rectify our particular faults.

Jesus finished with a wonderful invitation: 'Here I am! I stand at the door and knock. If anyone hears my voice and opens the door, I will come in and eat with him, and he with me.'[14] The reward offered is a celebratory feast. But we must first let him in.

In Holman Hunt's famous painting of this scene, Jesus stands, knocking at the door to someone's life. He wears a crown of thorns to remind us of the enormous price he paid on the cross to set us free. He holds a lantern to remind us of his wonderfully personal promise, 'I am the light of the world. Whoever follows me will never walk in darkness, but will have the light of life.'[15] The door itself has clearly never been opened – it is rusty, with ivy growing over it. Significantly, there's no handle on the *outside* of the door. Only we can open it from the inside.

So as Jesus knocks at the door of your life, will you open the door and let him come in? Will you let him put the final piece(s) of the jigsaw in place?

Remember that sense of longing for more we explored in the introduction? It's as though our loving heavenly Father has lots of gifts wrapped up with our name on, and he's waiting to give them to us. But it's as we put all the pieces of the jigsaw in place that we're able to unwrap the gifts.

- As we *believe* in him, we find we can trust him with our everyday worries and concerns, receiving his peace and joy.
- As we *belong* to his family, the church, we find a depth of friendship and love that takes us by surprise, and the privilege of being part of a community where everyone is equally valued.
- As we *behave* as Jesus wants us to, we find freedom to live as we were made to live and the power of God to change our lives for the better.
- As we are *baptized*, we feel the reassurance of God's great promises to us and know the celebration of God's kingdom.
- As we are *born again*, we know the certainty of God's Spirit within us, and the personal privilege of calling God 'my Father'.

If there are pieces missing in your jigsaw, you might find it helpful to use this sort of prayer:

My Father in heaven,
Thank you for the ways you've worked in my life so far.
I'm sorry for the ways I haven't completely followed your call
    on my life.
Please forgive me, especially for . . .
    [describe which bits of the jigsaw are missing or very faded]
I trust that Jesus died to pay for my sin.
Please come into my life in a new and deeper way.
By your Spirit, please transform me.

I want to put the missing pieces in place, with your help.
I want to live for you, from now on.
Amen.

There will be more things you need to do, depending on which pieces are missing. But praying that prayer is at least a step in the right direction. It's the start of a new adventure with God – enjoy it!

If you've prayed that prayer seriously, I'm so pleased that you're wanting to finish the puzzle – remember, the reward for completing this puzzle is infinitely more than £10,000! It's true life itself.

Questions for reflection

Read Matthew 7:15–27 from Jesus' Sermon on the Mount.

1. Jesus warns us about three groups of people (Christian leaders, keen Christians, and ordinary Christians) who claim to be Christians, but aren't. How are we supposed to spot fake Christians? What happens to them?
2. Look at the image of the jigsaw puzzle on page 127. Which of these pieces is definitely in place in your life? Thank God for that.
3. Are there any pieces where you're not sure if they're there or not (maybe it's as though they're drawn in pencil, not ink), or which are definitely *not* there? Talk to God about those pieces, and ask him to show you what to do to 'ink them in' or put them in place. Refer to the relevant chapters, if that helps.
4. If you've got all the pieces in place, read John 6:37–40 and Hebrews 10:22–23, which both speak of the assurance a

genuine Christian has. What *grounds* for assurance does a genuine Christian have? What are the *effects* of such assurance? What should it *prompt* the genuine Christian to do?

5. Glance back through the chapter. Talk to God in your own words about something that's challenged or encouraged you.

6. Is there someone else who you think might benefit from reading this book? Offer it to them!

Notes

Introduction: Unwrapping the jigsaw puzzle

1. John 10:10.
2. Good modern translations of the Bible include the New International Version (NIV), English Standard Version (ESV) and Contemporary English Version (CEV). Some may find *The Message* (a paraphrase of the Bible) helpful as an additional version. All of these and more can be read online at www.biblegateway.com, and may be purchased in good bookshops.

Piece 1: Believing

1. The *Daily Telegraph*, 22 March 2009, referring to an academic survey by Professor David Voas, published in *European Sociological Review*, vol. 25(2):155–168.
2. Many people think that 'science has disproved God' – but that's simply not true. For those interested in looking in more detail at the science–faith debate, there is a whole range of books available. See, for example, John Lennox, *God's Undertaker: Has Science Buried God?* (Lion Hudson, 2007); David Robertson, *The Dawkins Letters: Challenging Atheist Myths* (Christian Focus Publications, 2007); Alister McGrath, *Dawkins' God* (Wiley-Blackwell, 2004); Frances Collins, *The Language of God: A Scientist Provides Evidence for Belief* (Pocket Books, 2007).

3. E.g. John 5:23 and elsewhere.
4. John 14:9.
5. Matthew 22:37, where Jesus quoted from Deuteronomy 6:4–9.
6. John 6:25 (TNIV).
7. John 8:12.
8. Tom Wright, *Simply Christian* (SPCK, 2006), p. 116.
9. Matthew 5:48.
10. 1 Peter 2:22.
11. Luke 19:10 (CEV).
12. Mark 10:45.
13. Alister McGrath, *I Believe* (IVP, 1997), pp. 23–24.
14. John 6:37.
15. John 10:10.
16. John 6:28–29 (emphasis added).
17. John 3:16 (emphasis added).
18. John 3:18 (emphasis added).
19. John 20:31 (TNIV).
20. James 2:17.

Piece 2: Belonging

1. *Churchgoing in the UK* (Tearfund, April 2007).
2. Matthew 12:49–50.
3. John 13:34.
4. Galatians 6:10.
5. Ephesians 2:20–22 (CEV).
6. 1 Corinthians 12:12, 19 (CEV).
7. 1 Corinthians 12:27 (CEV).
8. John Stott, *The Living Church* (IVP, 2007), p. 19.
9. Research of seventy UK congregations conducted by Retail Maxim. Results published in *Word in Action* (Bible Society, Spring 2009).

10. Ephesians 4:16, emphasis added.
11. John Stott, *The Living Church* (IVP, 2007), pp. 19–20.
12. Ephesians 2:22.
13. 1 Peter 5:8.
14. Hebrews 10:25.
15. Rick Warren, *Why Getting Connected Matters* (pastors.com ministry toolbox, issue 371).
16. Revelation chapters 2 – 3.
17. John Stott, *The Message of Ephesians* (IVP, 1991), p. 126.
18. Romans 12:5.
19. Acts 2:42–47.
20. Acts 20:35.
21. Matthew 18:20.
22. Revelation 3:14–22.
23. John Stott, *Basic Christianity* (IVP, 1958), p. 123.
24. Matthew 13:24–30, 36–43, 47–50.
25. See Jesus' teaching in Matthew 7:15 and 24:11, picked up by the apostles later in the New Testament, e.g. Acts 20:29; 2 Peter 2:1; Jude 4.

Piece 3: Behaving

1. Matthew 5:22.
2. Matthew 5:28.
3. Matthew 5:44.
4. 'Bien sûr, il me pardonnera; c'est son métier.' A deathbed joke (1856), quoted in French by Sigmund Freud, *The Joke and its Relation to the Unconscious* (1905). Sourced from http://en.wikiquote.org/wiki/Heinrich_Heine on 23 July 2008.
5. 1 Timothy 1:16.
6. Dietrich Bonhoeffer, *The Cost of Discipleship* (first published 1937, reissued by SCM Press, 2001), p. 45.

7. Matthew 13:44.
8. Mark 8:34.
9. Romans 6:1–2.
10. Matthew 5:17.
11. Galatians 5:13–14.
12. 1 Timothy 1:8.
13. Psalm 19:8.
14. John 8:11.
15. Luke 19:8.
16. Isaiah 1:18.
17. Luke 14:28–30, 33 (TNIV).
18. Hebrews 11:25.
19. Mark 8:35 (TNIV).
20. John 10:10.
21. John 14:15.
22. 1 John 4:19.
23. 1 John 4:9 (emphasis added).
24. Jason Robinson, *Finding my Feet* (Hodder and Stoughton, 2003), p. 239.
25. 1 John 5:3.
26. Matthew 23:23–28.
27. John 13:25.
28. Leviticus 11:45 and elsewhere.
29. Matthew 5:48.
30. Matthew 25:31–46.
31. John 13:13.
32. Matthew 7:21–23, emphasis added. See also verses 24–27.
33. Bill Hybels, *The God You're Looking For* (Thomas Nelson, 1997), pp. 108–109.
34. Matthew 6:13.
35. Galatians 5:22–23.
36. Matthew 6:12.

37. 1 John 1:9.
38. Mark 12:29–31.

Piece 4: Baptism

1. Acts 22:16.
2. Isaiah 1:18.
3. Luke 12:50.
4. Luke 9:23.
5. Romans 6:3.
6. Michael Green, *Baptism* (Hodder and Stoughton, 1987), p. 49 (emphasis his).
7. 7. Romans 6:4–5 (TNIV).
8. J. I. Packer, *Concise Theology* (IVP, 1993), p. 212.
9. Galatians 3:27, emphasis added.
10. Matthew 28:19.
11. Acts 8:13–24.
12. Tom Wright, *Simply Christian* (SPCK, 2006), p. 183.
13. Acts 2:37–38, 41.
14. John Stott, *The Message of Acts* (IVP, 1990), p. 305.
15. This is what is affirmed publicly in a service of 'Confirmation' or 'Renewal of baptismal vows' or 'Believers' Baptism' – the exact pattern varying between denominations.
16. Sometimes referred to as 'baptism in the Spirit'.
17. Matthew 28:19.
18. As I've already indicated, the Salvation Army (almost uniquely in the world church) don't perform baptisms. As I understand it, their quibble with baptism isn't theological but pragmatic. One of the main reasons their founders chose not to baptize was because so many people at the time had been baptized as babies, but didn't develop a personal faith as adults, i.e. they felt the practice of baptism had become thoroughly devalued as

the symbol had been divorced from the reality. Instead, they developed a ceremony which they understand as equivalent to baptism (and take incredibly seriously), involving a clear profession of Christian faith and commitment to a lifestyle shaped by the Bible – but with no water involved. I wouldn't doubt that many committed members of the Salvation Army, who haven't been baptized with water, are indeed genuine Christians, although I don't agree with their position on water baptism.

19. Luke 23:42–43.
20. From J. I. Packer, *Growing in Christ* (Crossway, 2007).
21. Matthew 28:18–20.

Piece 5: Born again

1. It can be found in the conversation recorded in John 3:1–21.
2. John 3:3.
3. John 3:7.
4. John 3:5–6 (TNIV).
5. John 3:1.
6. See Numbers 21:4–9.
7. John 3:14–15.
8. John 3:8.
9. John 3:16, emphasis added.
10. John 10:10.
11. Philippians 4:7.
12. Philippians 4:12.
13. Romans 8:25.
14. 2 Corinthians 12:10.
15. Matthew 6:9.
16. John 15:15.
17. Simon Ponsonby, *More* (Kingsway, 2005), p. 13.

18. Billy Graham, *The Holy Spirit* (Word, 1988), quoted in Simon Ponsonby, *More*, p. 13.

Conclusion: Putting the pieces together

1. See www.christianityexplored.org or www.alpha.org for details of courses run at local churches.
2. Matthew 7:21–23.
3. Matthew 24:39–42.
4. Acts 10:1–2.
5. Galatians 5:7.
6. Galatians 4:15.
7. Galatians 5:4.
8. Revelation 3:2–3.
9. Matthew 25:32–33.
10. Revelation 20:12–15; see also Revelation 21:27.
11. Technically, Barack Obama was still 'President-Elect Obama' at the time of this story.
12. John 3:17.
13. All quotes from Revelation 3:16–20.
14. Revelation 3:20.
15. John 8:12.

Further reading

I don't pretend that a short book like this is the last word on any of the subjects covered. If you want to explore further, here are some suggestions.

Believing

Paul Little, *Know What You Believe* (IVP, 2008)
Alister McGrath, *I Believe: Exploring the Apostles' Creed* (IVP, 1997)
Michael Ots, *What Kind of God?* (IVP, 2008)
John Stott, *Basic Christianity* (IVP, 2008)
Tom Wright, *Simply Christian* (SPCK, 2006)

Belonging

Graham Beynon, *God's New Community* (IVP, 2005)
Simon Jones, *Why Bother with Church?* (IVP, 2001)
John Stott, *The Living Church* (IVP, 2007)

Behaving

John Chapman, *A Sinner's Guide to Holiness* (Matthias Media, 2005)
Tim Chester, *You Can Change* (IVP, 2008)

Julian Hardyman, *Maximum Life* (IVP, 2009)
John Piper, *Battling Unbelief* (IVP, 2008)
Vaughan Roberts, *Battles Christians Face* (Authentic, 2007)

Baptism

Stephen Gaukroger, *Being Baptised* (Scripture Union, 2003)
Michael Green, *Baptism* (Paternoster, 2006)

Born again

Graham Beynon, *Experiencing the Spirit* (IVP, 2006)
Mike Cain, *Real Life Jesus* (IVP, 2008)
John Piper, *Finally Alive* (Christian Focus, 2009)

Bible

No, I haven't suddenly added in another piece to the jigsaw! But throughout this book I've quoted from the Bible a lot, and it may be helpful to suggest some books which address questions arising from that:

Gordon Fee and Douglas Stewart, *How to Read the Bible for All its Worth* (Zondervan, third edition 2003)
Michael Green, *Bible Reading: A Beginner's Guide* (BRF, 2009)
Amy Orr-Ewing, *Why Trust the Bible?* (IVP, 2005)
John Stott, *Understanding the Bible* (Scripture Union, 2003)